PUBLIC HEALTH IN THE 21ST CENTURY

CREATING WELLNESS

AN INTEGRATIVE APPROACH

AN INTRODUCTION TO THE NATURAL APPROACH TO PREVENTIVE HEALTHCARE FOR FAMILIES, ATHLETES AND SENIORS

PUBLIC HEALTH IN THE 21ST CENTURY

Additional books in this series can be found on Nova's website under the Series tab.

Additional e-books in this series can be found on Nova's website under the e-book tab.

PUBLIC HEALTH IN THE 21ST CENTURY

CREATING WELLNESS

AN INTEGRATIVE APPROACH

AN INTRODUCTION TO THE NATURAL APPROACH TO PREVENTIVE HEALTHCARE FOR FAMILIES, ATHLETES AND SENIORS

JOHN L. STUMP
DONNA RETZLAFF-ROBERTS
DAVID P. SNIEZEK

nova publishers
New York

NOTICE TO THE READER

Library of Congress Cataloging-in-Publication Data

ISBN: 978-1-63463-837-1

Library of Congress Control Number: 2015940903

Published by Nova Science Publishers, Inc. † New York

This book is dedicated to our family, patients, colleagues and friends. Thank you for your care, help and support that allow us to pursue the passion of Wellness and health care. We are writing to share the knowledge and wisdom that we have gained over the years from the many parts of the world our education has taken us

CONTENTS

PREFACE

Physicians are well trained in conventional medicine and most are well acquainted with Integrative Medicine, which incorporates conventional and alternative medical practices in a complementary manner. However, many patients are less understanding of what Integrative Medicine is and when it should be used.

This book is intended for the untrained person who wants to become more knowledgeable about Integrative Medicine, where the objective is to treat the whole person (mind, body and spirit) and make more informed decisions regarding his or her own medical care. It is an introduction to complimentary, alternative, integrative and even anti-aging and functional medicines tailored to aid the patient's personal needs and goals for health and wellness. This symbiotic relationship between different disciplines is accomplished simply by putting wellness first in our thinking instead of sickness and disease.

Most people only think about health when it's lost; many times, this is too late! Don't let the first heart, stroke or lower back attack happen. Take wellness and preventive steps to improve your health status now and read this book!

Keywords: integrative medicine, prevention, alternative medicine, complementary medicine and wellness

Chapter I

INTRODUCTION

"Happiness depends upon one's self"

ARISTOTLE (384-322 BC)

WHAT IS INTEGRATIVE WELLNESS?

Integrative Medicine and wellness is the future of health care in our country. Individuals who specialize in integrative wellness incorporate conventional and alternative medical practices in a complementary manner, where the objective is to treat the whole person; mind, body and sprit (emotional). Alternative medical practices can include acupuncture, chiropractic, Traditional Chinese Medicine, herbs, psychology, physical therapy, massage, homeopathy, and naturopathy. By utilizing both conventional and alternative medical practices in a complementary manner, Integrative Medicine puts wellness first rather than focusing on sickness and disease. Health care professionals who practice Integrative Medicine can include those who are trained in conventional medicine (such as medical doctors and nurse practitioners), as well as those trained in alternative practices. Regardless of the specialty, each supplements and complements their specialty by applying the techniques best suited to achieving the patient's wellness. Some practitioners use the term *Functional Medicine* or *Anti-Aging Medicine* instead of Integrative Medicine. All of these types of practices involve focusing on prevention instead of treating illness once it arises.

Scientific, clinical and laboratory diagnostic methods (evidenced based) assist the practitioner to see underlying causes of the condition. The practitioner seeks to detect physiological imbalances and employ early intervention prior to the condition manifesting as an illness. By educating patients on the importance of wellness and prevention, a greater number of individuals can stay well, become healthier, and avoid expensive, invasive, disease-based interventions to care for the condition.

Pharmaceutical or Natural

For well over one hundred years now, the "paradigm" of pharmaceutical superiority has been pushed by big business and private enterprise. A paradigm is very resistant to change, since the human tendency is to hold on to a belief for as long as possible, even when new discoveries challenge it. As more discoveries come forward and evidence continues to mount, however, we are eventually forced to make a "paradigm shift," in which we find it necessary to replace our old paradigm with a new one.

Today, we are on the verge of a paradigm shift in our view of and attitude toward health and health care. Our disease-oriented paradigm in the past one hundred years is gradually giving way to a new health-oriented, wellness one. Like all paradigms, the old one is resistant to change, but even more so in this case because of the special interests that reap trillion dollar profits from the present paradigm! Special interests spend millions of dollars each day to keep the old medical paradigm in place.

It is important to realize this new paradigm did not originate within the medical system, it has been forced upon a less than willing medical establishment by the people – people who have grown tired of watching their health and their life savings dwindle while drug companies continue to reap billions in profits.

A PARADIGM SHIFT

The new health paradigm – the paradigm in which prevention and wellness is considered better than a cure; in which the *innate* healing power of the body is recognized and supported; in which doctors function as teachers not demigods; and in which we, the people, are to play a greater role in the decisions that will affect our health and wellness.

This is not to say that medicine and medication do not have their rightful place in the health care system. When there is an accident with profuse bleeding, broken bones, and or lacerations or there is an acute illness like appendicitis, flu, Ebola or any such conditions - the nearest emergency room, hospital or medical clinic should be the immediate destination. There, MD's can do what they are trained better than anyone in the world to do… crisis-oriented care. However, when it comes to chronic degenerative disease such as arthritis, cancer prevention, stroke prevention, diabetes, or obesity there are other alternatives. This is where Prevention comes into play and individuals need to take responsibility for their own life style choices. If the individual does nothing to protect their health and continues through life waiting for a crisis like a heart attack, stroke or other infirmity from a poor lifestyle before acting, then it's the individual and not the health care system that has failed. Failed in the basic human responsibility, to educate and to take as much responsibility for maintaining your body's health as you would your automobile. This is what the new paradigm is all about- health responsibility!

HOLISTIC CENTERED HEALTH CARE

This is a whole person, patient centered approach to health care, rather than the traditional disease-centered, isolated-set-of-symptoms approach used in the past. There may be three or four specialty practitioners working together who offer their expertise for the benefit of their patients. One has to always look at the whole person and not just consider the symptoms, regardless of whether the symptoms involve digestive, immune, endocrine, energy, musculoskeletal, nervous, emotional or any other single set of health characteristics.

Doctors who practice this way realize the individual's health throughout life is on a continuum or a spectrum. At one end, there's optimal well-being, at the opposite end, chronic disease; such as heart disease, stroke, cancer, diabetes and obesity that are at epidemic levels now in our society. We must understand there is no perfect health state. Everyone gets sick or doesn't feel well from time to time. Variation is the essence of life, and the human might be the ultimate example. This why we must not get angry or depressed when we fall victim to accident, virus, bacteria, etc., We are only human and have to live in this world as an anthropological being subject to the laws of the universe like everything else. It is normal to be sick from time to time but we want to strive to have the occurrence in as few and as short a duration as possible.

Always remember, healing comes from within. It's your body's innate wisdom to seek balance of mind, body and spirit. When symmetry and equilibrium is lost the status of health is in jeopardy in our mind, body and spirit (remember the holistic being) and we begin to slip toward the sickness end of the scale.

THE WELLNESS CONTINUUM

For far too long it has been taught that there's no middle ground. Either a person is healthy or diseased; the organ is either well or sick. Yet, there is a middle ground or "gray zone" where organs can become weak, stressed, rundown, toxic and move to the pathologic and diseased end of the scale or they can become stronger, more vital, and healthier and move to the wellness end of the spectrum.

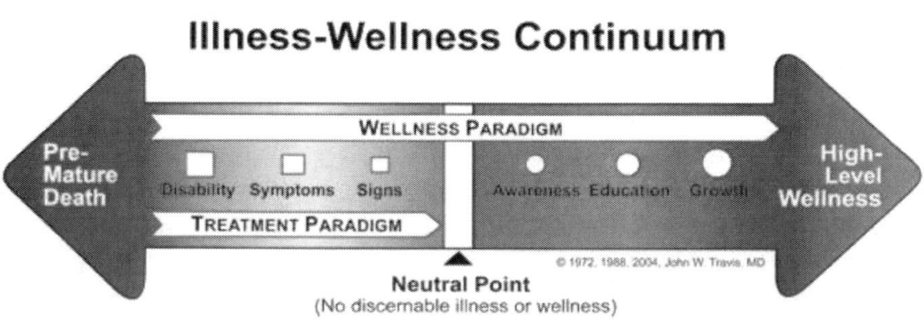

Figure 1. The Wellness Continuum.

When organs become sick, there's a host of symptoms that manifest themselves. Without the integrative model, these problems are usually treated symptomatically usually with pharmaceuticals. For instance, gas, bloating, migraines, neck, low back pain, menstrual pain and hormone imbalances all are signs of organ dysfunction in the "gray zone" discussed earlier.

Up until recently everything in medicine was a "specialty" area. The Neurologist (Brain and Spinal Cord), ENT (Ear, Nose and Throat), Cardiologist (Heart and vascular system), Pulmonologist (Lung), Gastroenterologist (Digestive), Orthopaedist (Bones and Joints), and Chiropractors (Spine), Podiatrist (feet), etc., are part of the myriad of practitioners whose philosophy it is to hunt and treat disease and conditions of their area. One of the most important things Integrative Wellness has taught us is 'wholeness' of the individual and to think about the whole person.

INDIVIDUALISM IN HEALTH CARE

At the same time we must remember every person is an individual and may not fall into a certain category. An individual may be in a roomful of sick people and still not catch the bacteria, virus, fungus or parasite that they are exposed to. Yet that same person will have some other weak link in their defensive chain. It may be they are colorblind or have a weak stomach or have psoriatic arthritis. In our nearly 50 years in the healing arts we have never seen or heard of an individual who has perfect health all the time. There are legends and fables of people living to be 300 years old. Yes, the body could conceivably live that long if taken care of, but we humans must live in this world and in this environment that has become toxic to the tissues in a manner of speaking. Also, some aging specialists feel we humans are limited by the length of our telomeres (the ends of our chromosomes), which have been linked to the aging process and life extension possibilities. Let's suffice it to say that wellness and prevention methods and guidelines follow the same projections, as do life extension and aging specialist.

WE ARE STRIVING FOR WELLNESS … NOT SICKNESS CARE

It has become common for people to live past one-hundred years. As a matter of fact you may have been in a waiting room with one or more of these centenarians. These are the escapers, the people who escape serious illness all their lives, which is about 1 in every 100,000 people. They usually range from

100 to 110, as not many people live beyond 110. However, there are now several over the age of 110 in the world which means it may be possible to stretch the boundaries of life to 125 with the proper wellness and prevention emphasis according to the aging specialists call gerontologists.

We know of a case where the patient was 109 and the oldest among her nursing home residents. She contracted herpes zoster (commonly known as shingles) and chose to fight it with acupuncture and nutrition, and was successful. However, the case did take longer to control due to her immune system being a little weaker and compromised due to her extended age. Then there was Miss Irma, who at 104 had never worn glasses, still had her own teeth, had outlived several husbands, took no medication and survived alone in her home until a fall caused her to break a hip one month before her 105th birthday.

When she was young, Miss Irma had been a patient of Dr. B.J. Palmer, the dynamic son of the founder of Chiropractic. She said “Dr. Palmer saved me from life in a wheelchair and the awful pain after being thrown from a mule when I was very young.” Before WWII she left the U.S. and went to Costa Rica to establish a Quaker religious colony. She lived there many years and helped build the town that is today the city of Monte Verde. Her entire life was dedicated to a righteous and spiritual life of healthy and friendly relationships with all people.

Miss Irma moved back to the U.S. at the age of 75 to be close to some of her grandchildren. She went to a chiropractic office and said she was looking for a DC (Doctor of Chiropractic) from Palmer College who could adjust the spine, and would be interested in her health rather than in her disease. This insight in prevention and wellness is very impressive. She told the doctor “I'm interested in staying healthy and would like to come in once a month for what she called, a "tune-up.” She may remind you of someone you have known who is your grandmother or great-grandmother's age. In our opinion, every person at 99 years of age should get a card like a “Get out of Jail Free Card” in Monopoly that would allow them to get free medical care. They have lived a life of prevention and deserve a few breaks from the health care system.

There is one more octogenarian we want to introduce. He became a patient at the age of 90. He told the receptionist at the clinic that he had never been to a doctor as an adult, took no medication and had no external aids such as a hearing aid, false teeth, glasses or cane. He lived alone since his wife had died nearly 15 years earlier. He was a retired math professor from Tuskegee University in Alabama. He remembered getting the childhood diseases but couldn't remember being seriously ill as an adult. He reportedly had adopted the study and practice of yoga while doing graduate study in India. He said his yoga teacher had emphasized how important proper breathing is to health and longevity and how he had continued yoga all these years.

There is now a "modified yoga" called "chair yoga, a class for seniors." He had come to investigate the class. He emphasized that he had gotten colds and minor illness in the past 50 years and wanted to stay as healthy as possible. At 90 he came to our clinic and he is now 101. He said "He was seeking preventive care and wellness… what patients say we advertise… by being examples." We try to say this many times in many ways, but to hear a patient come in and say these words makes you feel like you are doing your part to present wellness and prevention in everyone's daily life!

Types of Practitioners

There are many types of health care providers with a variety of titles, training, and skills. Let us review the various types with a brief description of each so that the terms and acronyms have been defined.

Medical Doctor (MD)

A physician. Someone who has graduated from medical school (usually 4 years) and completed further years of training as a "resident" or "intern" under the supervision of an experienced MD. Residency duration varies by specialty, but is a minimum of 3 years and up to 8 years for some surgical specialties. Might be primary care physician or a specialist. Primary Care physicians are commonly referred to as General Practitioners (GP) and might be trained either in Family Practice or Internal Medicine (an "Internist").

Doctor of Osteopathic Medicine (DO)

A medical doctor who takes a holistic approach, uses manipulation methods and combines conventional with alternative medicine. Also referred to as an Osteopath.

Doctor of Chiropractic (DC)

A Chiropractor or one who practices Chiropractic. A form of alternative medicine that deals with the neuromusculoskeletal system. Chiropractic will be covered in much greater detail later.

Doctor of Oriental (DOM) or Oriental Medicine Doctor (OMD)

One who practices Traditional Chinese Medicine that includes acupuncture and herbal medicine. Acupuncture will be covered in much greater detail later. The acronym OMD is primarily used in the East, while DOM is primarily used in the West.

Physical Therapist (PT) or Doctor of Physical Therapy (DPT)

A health care profession dealing with restoring motor abilities that have been lost or impaired. Treatment involves non-invasive movement and mechanical force. Whether or not someone has a doctorate in physical therapy depends on the amount of formal education they have had.

Physician Assistant (PA)

Training is a condensed form of Medical School (2-3 years). There is no residency, but must work under the supervision of a qualified MD. Can diagnose, treat, prescribe medications, and assist in surgery within their scope of practice.

Nurse Practitioner (NP)

A nurse who has advanced training beyond a Registered Nurse. Qualified to diagnose, order treatment, and prescribe medications within their scope of practice.

Acupuncturist

An acupuncturist may or may not be a Doctor of Oriental Medicine (see above). One who has been trained in acupuncture but not in herbal medicine is an Acupuncturist and not a DOM. Acupuncture will be covered in much greater detail later.

Herbalist

An herbal practitioner has been trained in herbal medicine. Note that Doctors or Oriental Medicine are trained in herbal medicine, but an Herbalist is not necessarily a DOM.

Massage Therapist

One who has been trained and licensed in massage therapy. The amount of training and the licensing requirements differ by state. Massage will be covered in greater detail later.

Homeopath

One who practices homeopathy or homeopathic medicine which is based on the principle "like cures like." This will be covered in greater detail later.

Naturopath

Naturopathy includes a broad array of natural practices which can include homeopathy, herbalism, acupuncture, nutrition and lifestyle counseling. This will be covered in greater detail later.

Psychologist

One has graduate education in psychology. A Clinical Psychologist usually has a PhD as well as clinical training and counsels patients on emotional and mental issues.

Nutritionist

One who is educated in nutrition. The term is somewhat widely used and education may range from someone who took a few classes to someone who has a PhD in nutrition. Nutrition will be covered in detail later.

Ayurvedic Practitioner

Ayurvedic medicine or Ayurveda is a holistic practice that was developed in India thousands of years ago. It is based on the principle of promoting wellness via the balance of body, mind, and spirit. Treatments can include meditation, yoga, stretching, massage, aroma therapy, herbs and supplements, and lifestyle changes.

Chapter II

EVOLUTION OF HEALTH CARE

Dr. David Sniezek, DC, MD, LAcup, FAAIM, FAAMA

Everyone thinks of changing the world, but no one thinks of changing himself.
-- Leo Tolstoy

Until recently in the U.S. the healthcare system was more like a medical care system with emphasis on diagnosis and treatment of illness rather than a healthcare system that also included prevention and wellness. This section will review the development of Integrative Medicine (IM) as an approach to wellness and healing in the U.S. healthcare system over the past several decades and explore examples of how Integrative Medicine, specifically medical acupuncture, has been used successfully in traditional medical specialties.

The birth, growth, and subsequent incorporation of IM into the U.S. health care system are the result of many factors including a healthcare system in crisis, slow economy and a dysfunctional political system. These factors created a window of opportunity for a new system that addressed many of the shortcomings of the medical care system. For instance, traditional medicine placed the physician at the center of importance and power. Diagnostic and treatment options were often made with minimal concern for or input from patients or their families. One of the major principles of Integrative Medicine practice is placing the patient on equal footing or at least having a major role in the decision making process. Once this simple principle was put into practice, healthcare organizations (HCO) and private practices noticed improved patient and family satisfaction surveys. Improved patient satisfaction bolstered patient participation, which, in turn, improved functional outcome measures.

This section will briefly discuss how our healthcare system, economics and politics provided a unique opportunity for Integrative Medicine to take hold and flourish. It will then explore examples of two areas of specialized medicine, oncology and sports medicine, which have successfully incorporated Integrative Medicine into their practices.

THE UNITED STATES HEALTH CARE CRISIS

The United States is experiencing a health care crisis for which there is no single cause or simple solution. Here is a short list of some of the major issues threatening our country's health care.

- *Chronic diseases, poor nutrition, inactivity, and tobacco use are causing serious health problems* – including Type II diabetes, heart disease, stroke, and cancer – now, and if left unchecked, will lead to worsening conditions in the future [1, 2, 3] It is estimated that health care costs for chronic disease treatment account for over 75% of national health expenditures.[4]
- *Lack of sustainable cost control measures.* The major drivers of healthcare costs include technology and prescription drugs, chronic

[1] CDC.gov. 2014 Surgeon General's Report: The Health Consequences of Smoking – 50 Years of Progress. (Retrieved November 28, 2014) http://www.cdc.gov/tobacco/data_statistics/sgr/50th-anniversary/index.htm#report

[2] CDC.gov. The Power of Prevention. Chronic Disease…the Public Health Challenge of the 21st Century. (Retrived November 28, 2014) http://www.cdc.gov/chronicdisease/pdf/2009-power-of-prevention.pdf

[3] Goeppinger J, Barnwell S, Ensley D. Complete Projects Comparisons of Outcomes North Carolina. (Retrieved November 18, 2014) http://www.cdc.gov/arthritis/funded_science/completed/ashc_cdsmp_unc.htm

[4] CDC.gov. Rising Health Care Costs Unsustainble. (Retrived November 28, 2014) http://www.cdc.gov/workplacehealthpromotion/businesscase/reasons/rising.html

disease, aging of the population, and administrative costs. Control of these influences continues to elude lawmakers.[5]

- *Anticipated shortage of healthcare workforce* – There is a critical shortage of healthcare professionals in the U.S. that will increase dramatically by at least 124,000 physicians and 500,000 nurses by 2025, just as the aging population and the nation's ongoing population growth are placing greater demands on the health care system.[6]

According to a 2010 New England Journal of Medicine article, there are 456,000 preventable deaths annually in the United States from smoking, 395,000 from high blood pressure, 216,000 from obesity, 191,000 from inactivity, 190,000 from high blood sugar, and 113,000 from high cholesterol.[7, 8]

One-third of Americans are overweight, another third are obese, and a fifth smoke. We consume too much processed foods and do not exercise enough. Physical activity of children has been shown to decline from three hours per day at age nine to less than an hour by age 15. In spite of being first for per capita spending on health care, the U.S. ranks 39th for infant mortality, 43rd for female mortality, 42nd for male mortality, and 36th for life expectancy.[9]

Today, the United States has a medical care system rather than a health care system. The medical model's emphasis is placed on treating illness instead of placing effort and resources in prevention. The word "prevention" derives from two Latin roots that mean "before" and "come." By anticipating harm, we can take action to stop it, avert it, or minimize its effects.

Prevention is valuable at any age. Fewer hospitalizations, shorter lengths of stay for those who are hospitalized, and a drop in unplanned readmissions within 30 days from 24% to under 10% can be accomplished with some simple but powerful preventative measures. These include the use of electronic

---

[5] Orszag, PR. CBO Testimony. Growth in Health Care Costs. January 31, 2008 (Retrieved November 28, 2014) http://www.cbo.gov/sites/default/files/01-31-healthtestimony.pdf

[6] Zywiak, W., U.S. Healthcare Workforce Shortages: Caregivers. (Retrieved November 28, 2014) http://assets1.csc.com/health_services/downloads/CSC_US_Healthcare_Workforce_Shortages_Caregivers.pdf

[7] Danaei G, Ding EL, Mozaffarian D, et al. The preventable causes of death in the United States: comparative risk assessment of dietary, lifestyle, and metabolic risk factors. PLoS Med 2009;6(4):e1000058.

[8] Christopher J.L. Murray, M.D., D.Phil., and Julio Frenk, M.D., Ph.D., M.P.H. Ranking 37th—Measuring the Performance of the U.S. Health Care System.
N Engl J Med 2010; 362:98-99. January 14, 2010 DOI: 10.1056/NEJMp0910064

[9] Doe J. WHO Statistical Information System (WHOSIS). Geneva: World Health Organization, September 2009.

medical records, more nurses to assist with care coordination, increased number of visits to each hospitalized patient, and an automatic office visit within 72 hours of a hospital discharge.

U.S. Economic and Political Environment

In budgets reviewed by the Congressional Budget Office (CBO) benefits for prevention were not measured clearly because the CBO's cost benefit analysis only took into consideration five years from the time of implementation. It is well known that most preventative programs' benefits could not be quantified until decades after implementation. With passage of the Patient Protection and Affordable Care Act (PPACA) in 2010 there was an increase in funding level for Integrative Medicine from $500 million in 2010 to $2 billion annually starting in 2015, with a total of $15 billion from 2010 to 2020. This is clear evidence that Integrative Medicine has entered the mainstream discussion of health and wellness and is more seriously being considered as an approach for addressing escalating healthcare costs.[10] Other economic and political concerns are the anticipated shortage of healthcare workforce and the lack of sustainable cost control measures.[11] The President's Council of Economic Advisors says that health care dominates the list of industries that are projected to add the most jobs through 2016.[12]

Prevention

From the perspective of the U.S. healthcare system, Integrative Medicine has its roots in prevention. Preventative healthcare consists of measures taken for disease prevention, as opposed to disease treatment.[13] Just as health

[10] Walsh, Taylor. Tom Harkin on Integrative Medicine & Health. *Getting to Integrative Health & Wellness*. April 25, 2011. http://gettingto.wordpress.com/2011/04/25/tom-harkin-on-integrative-medicine-health/, Retrieved December 6, 2014.

[11] National Health Care Worthforce, 2014. (Retrieved November 28, 2014). http://www.aafp.org/advocacy/informed/workforce/nhcwc.html

[12] 2011 Annual Report to Congresson Whitehouse Staff. http://www.whitehouse.gov/briefing-room/disclosures/annual-records/2011

[13] Katz, D., & Ather, A. 2009. Preventive Medicine, Integrative Medicine & The Health of The Public. Commissioned for the IOM Summit on Integrative Medicine and the Health of the Public. Retrieved December 6, 2014 fromhttp://www.iom.edu/~/media/Files/Activity

encompasses a variety of physical and mental states, so do disease and disability, which are affected by the environment, genetics, disease agents, and lifestyle choices. Health, disease, and disability are dynamic processes that begin before individuals realize they are affected.

Preventive healthcare strategies are typically described as taking place at the primary, secondary, and tertiary prevention levels. In the 1940s, Hugh R. Leavell and E. Gurney Clark coined the term primary prevention. They worked at the Harvard and Columbia University Schools of Public Health, respectively, and they later expanded the levels to include secondary and tertiary prevention.[14] Goldston (1987) notes that these levels might be better described as "prevention, treatment, and rehabilitation" though the terms primary, secondary, and tertiary prevention are still commonly in use today. [15]

In spite of these known benefits, many businesses as well as educational and governmental institution have been slow in incorporating integrative health practices and prevention into their organizations and communities.[16] During the 1970s and 80s there had been more public awareness of the shortcomings of traditional medicine even during times of illness. People with cancer were going to Mexico to received “alternative” treatments, such as Laetrile. The U.S. healthcare crisis, economic and political environment, and failure of traditional medicine to fill the growing needs and awareness of the patient developed fertile ground for new direction in medicine. Enter Integrative Medicine.

Integrative Medicine

Integrative Medicine is an established movement in North America and China. It is also a developing movement in parts of the Middle East and

%20Files/Quality/IntegrativeMed/Preventive%20Medicine%20Integrative%20Medicine%20and%20the%20Health%20of%20the%20Public.pdf

[14] Hugh R. Leavell and E. Gurney Clark as "the science and art of preventing disease, prolonging life, and promoting physical and mental health and efficiency. Leavell, H. R., & Clark, E. G. (1979). Preventive Medicine for the Doctor in his Community (3rd ed.). Huntington, NY: Robert E. Krieger Publishing Company.

[15] Goldston, S. E. (Ed.). (1987). Concepts of primary prevention: A framework for program development. Sacramento: California Department of Mental Health.

[16] TowersWatson.com. 2009/2010. The Health and Productivity Advantage. (Retrieved November 28, 2014) http://webcache.googleusercontent.com/search?q=cache:CoOpJ7uhQvoJ:https://www.towerswatson.com/DownloadMedia.aspx%3Fmedia%3D%257B12AC8E91-D884-435D-A7F4-86603314F443%257D+&cd=1&hl=en&ct=clnk&gl=us&client=safari

continental Europe, especially Scandinavia. Patients want "... a knowledgeable physician with an inclusive medical armamentarium who could, as appropriate, draw on various medical models to facilitate their health and healing."[17] Integrative medicine also stresses the importance of lifestyle. According to Andrew Weil, MD,

> Health and disease result from interactions between genes and all aspects of lifestyle, including diet, physical activity, rest and sleep, stress, and quality of relationships, work and so forth. Lifestyle choices may influence disease risks more than genes and must be a focus of the medical history. Lifestyle medicine, which is one component of IM, gives physicians information and tools to enable them to prevent and treat disease more effectively.[18]

Andrew Weil further defines Integrative Medicine as the rational, evidence-based combination of conventional therapy with complementary interventions into an individualized therapeutic regimen that addresses the whole person.[19] In essence, IM is a conservative approach that seeks to restore the core values of the profession, including such ancient precepts as Hippocrates' pledge to "first do no harm" and "to value the healing power of nature." IM favors less invasive and drastic treatments whenever possible. Integrative Medicine is also fiscally conservative and relies on less expensive technology and more on simpler methods, given the circumstances of illness. A comparison of the current medical practice compared to an integrative approach can be seen on the "Transformation Chart" shown here in Table 1.

Another critical component of IM is the concept of "shared decision-making." In order to ensure that each patient gets the treatment that is right for him or her, the choice should be a shared decision, involving both the patient and the clinician. In the process known as "shared decision-making," the patient is a fully informed partner in the choice, knowledgeable about the risk and benefit trade-offs of each treatment option. According to the Dartmouth Atlas Project 2011, "When done right, shared decision-making results in a better decision: a personalized choice based on both the best scientific evidence and the patient's own values."[20]

---

[17] Coulter ID, Ellison, MA, Hilton L, Rhodes HJ, Ryan G. Hospital-Based Integrative Medicine – A Case Study of the Barriers and Factors Facilitating the Creation of a Center. RAND Corporation. 2008; (Retrieved November 28, 2014) http://www.rand.org/content/dam/rand/pubs/monographs/2007/RAND_MG591.pdf

[18] Weil A, Abrams D. Integrative Oncology. Oxford Press. NY. 2008. p2.

[19] Weil A, Abrams D. Integrative Oncology. Oxford Press. NY. 2008. p2.

[20] Dartmouth Atlas Project 2011. (Retrieved November 28, 2014) http://www.dartmouthatlas.org

Table 1. Transformational Chart[21]

Current Medical Practice evolving to...	Integrative Medicine Practice
Health is most often considered to be the absence of disease.	Health is seen as a vital state of physical, mental, emotional, social and spiritual wellbeing, which enables a person to be engaged in life.
The physician tends to act as the authority figure.	The physician acts as a partner in the patient's care.
The patient is encouraged to follow the physician's directions.	The empowered and informed patient is an integral part of the decision-making process.
The interventions are often directed only towards the treatment of a specific disease or trauma.	The interventions are designed to treat the illness as well as the whole person, addressing the physical, mental, emotional, social and spiritual factors that influence health and disease.
A patient's stress level is not always taken into consideration or treated.	Patients are taught how to recognize, manage and decrease stress.
A patient's dietary habits are largely ignored.	Patients are given nutritional counseling; food is understood to have a significant influence on health and disease.
Social determinants of health such as unemployment, abuse, neglect, and financial status are not always given full consideration.	Social determinants of health such as unemployment, abuse, neglect, and financial status are considered in the care.
Environmental influences are rarely addressed.	Environmental influences on health and healing are investigated, considered and addressed in the care process.
Care is not always coordinated across providers.	Care is coordinated across providers.
Health plans are rarely created.	Each patient is given an individualized health plan based on his or her unique needs and circumstances.
Many decisions are based on the needs of the health care system.	Decisions are based on the needs of the patient.
Prevention and health promotion are not always practiced.	Prevention and health promotion are emphasized.
Only conventional interventions are considered.	The care makes use of all appropriate therapeutic approaches.

[21] The Bravewell Collaborative. Integrative Medicine: Improving Health Care for Patients and Health Care Delivery for Providers and Payors. Minneapolis, Minnesota 55404. (Retrieved December 17, 2014) http://www.bravewell.org/content/pdf/IntegrativeMedicine2.pdf , 2010, pg 10.

Finally, there is an abundance of high-quality medical evidence for health and cost savings benefit for implementing appropriate lifestyle changes for conditions such as diabetes, obesity, heart disease, as well as lung, breast and prostate cancer.[22] Integrative Medicine is evidence-based conventional and alternative treatments that take into account the whole person (body, mind, and spirit), including all aspects of lifestyle. It emphasizes the therapeutic relationship and makes use of all appropriate therapies, both conventional and complementary. The principles of Integrative Medicine as established by Dr. Andrew Weil, the founder of IM, are listed below[23]:

- A partnership between patient and practitioner in the healing process
- Appropriate use of conventional and alternative/complementary methods to facilitate the body's innate healing response
- Consideration of all factors that influence health, wellness and disease, including mind, spirit and community as well as body
- A philosophy that neither rejects conventional medicine nor accepts alternative therapies uncritically
- Recognition that good medicine should be based in good science, be inquiry driven, and be open to new paradigms
- Use of natural, effective, less-invasive interventions whenever possible
- Use of the broader concepts of promotion of health and the prevention of illness as well as the treatment of disease
- Training of practitioners to be models of health and healing, committed to the process of self-exploration and self-development

THE BUSINESS OF INTEGRATIVE MEDICINE

Integrative Medicine revenues represent 2% of the $2.5T spent annually on national healthcare, and there are estimates of a doubling in sales of integrative practitioner products and services from roughly $25B to nearly $50B from 1999 to 2010. According to the American Hospital Association, "...

[22] CDC.gov. The Power of Prevention. Chronic Disease...the Public Health Challenge of the 21st Century. (Retrived November 28, 2014) http://www.cdc.gov/chronicdisease/pdf/2009-power-of-prevention.pdf

[23] DrWeil.com. http://www.drweil.com/drw/u/ART02054/Andrew-Weil-Integrative-Medicine.html

42 percent of responding hospitals indicated they offer one or more complementary and alternative medicine (CAM) therapies, up from 37 percent in 2007." Furthermore, according to the National Center for Complementary and Alternative Medicine, 40% of the U.S. population spent nearly $34B on out-of-pocket complementary and alternative therapies and products during 2007 alone.[24]

[24] NCCAM.nih.gov. (Retrieved December 17, 2014). http://nccam.nih.gov/health/whatiscam

Chapter III

INTEGRATIVE PRACTICE

"The greatest revolution in our generation is the discovery that human beings, by changing the inner attitudes of their minds, can change the outer aspects of their lives."

WILLIAM JAMES (1842-1910)

WHEN ONE NEEDS CARE

When an individual does move to the sick side of the health continuum for a short period of time the person needs to understand their condition, what they need to do and whom they should seek advice from.

Something has caused the patient to go beyond the prevention boundary of their body's immune system. The patient should start with the most knowledgeable of the medical professionals about general medical care, the General Practitioner (GP) whose specialty may be Family Medicine or Internal Medicine. When a person feels sick, they want and need help to identify the problem area and their status.

The GP is then faced with the choice and responsibility of educating the patient in addition to diagnosing and treating the patient for the acute health care crisis in which they find themselves. All too often the mainstream medical model is for the GP to look toward pharmaceuticals and possible surgery to 'cure' the disease or correct the symptom, which may correct the problem in the short term. However, this does nothing to educating the patient on how to prevent the condition and work long term toward a wellness lifestyle mode of correction.

The patient benefits when the GP is knowledgeable about the benefits of Integrative Medicine and how a holistic approach can help patients. When a patient is sick or in pain and visits the GP, this ideal scenario can be summarized as:

1) Diagnose
2) Counsel
3) Treat
4) Follow-up

The second step (Counsel) is all too often skipped. Here the patient should be counseled and educated about the importance of a better lifestyle. If the patient does not follow through on the proper life style changes, then the patient is choosing which end of the scale they wish to dwell in.

In the third step (Treat) the physician brings in other health care practitioners as needed based on the patient's condition. In taking an integrative approach this may include conventional practitioners (physician specialists) and/or alternative practitioners. In the past GP's frequently did not consider alternatives outside of conventional medicine, but the perspective in the medical community is changing and many physicians are now utilizing alternative interventions before crisis medicine or surgery is needed. These alternative specialties may include psychology (emotional), chiropractic/ applied kinesiology (structural), acupuncture/Chinese Medicine (functional), nutrition and homeopathy (biochemical), physical medicine and physical therapy (physical), and massage/bodywork (energy/touch). These specialties are prepared to work with your medical doctor or your cancer specialist in order to contribute to the patient's health and wellbeing. The problem had been that many medical doctors were unwilling to work with those outside of traditional medicine, but this perspective is changing. Millions of people are now going to alternative interventions before crisis medicine or surgery is needed.

There are similarities that run through all natural health philosophies and these are what are focused on with Integrative Health Care. The most fundamental tenet of Integrative philosophy is, *the body has capacity to heal itself*, under the correct circumstances. Those "correct circumstance" are what practitioners try to create for the patient. The correct health environment for the body, mind and spirit is needed to create the happiness and harmony leading to total health and wellness.

LIKE MINDED PROFESSIONALS

In an ideal situation a group of like-minded medical professionals would work together in a clinic. These could include the following:

- MD - Medical Doctor
- DO - Doctor of Osteopathic Medicine
- DC - Doctor of Chiropractic
- DOM - Doctor of Oriental Medicine Doctor
- PT - Physical Therapist (or DPT - Doctor of Physical Therapy)
- ND - Naturopathy Doctor
- NP - Nurse Practitioner

Unfortunately there are state and local laws in many areas that prevent different specialties from practicing together. In addition, it would be beneficial if more of these specialties were able to prescribe pain medication, anti-inflammatories, and muscle relaxants to alleviate patients' discomfort. However, for now only the MD and the DO can prescribe in all 50 states.

Yet, the Nurse Practitioner has found a unique niche in the healing arts world. They are now able to work both with and independent of the Medical Doctor. At one time they could only do what the MD had ordered them to do but now there is more latitude for independent thinking on the part of the Nurse Practitioner. The Nurse Practitioner has for decades seen both the upside and the downside to allopathic practice. Allopathic refers to conventional medicine's reliance on pharmacology and surgery. They have seen how pharmaceutics take the dominate position in every health care case when other methods could have been utilized and monies saved. Today, Nurse Practitioners are taking on a new leadership role in the prevention and wellness arena. They understand that it saves lives and dollars when prevention and lifestyle changes can be used instead of a prescription. This is why we feel as time goes on and the wellness and prevention scene unfolds the Nurse Practitioner will play a prominent role.

The DC, DOM, DPT and other alternative health care practitioners can rest assured and realize that this integrative model does not in any way reshape, change or minimize the basic philosophical foundation of any practitioner or allied care where natural methods are used. This model of integrative health care offers a truly ultimate alternative approach to wellness by giving each individual patient the option to choose the most natural non-invasive methodology offered in preventative care. This concept is what was termed "the patient centered philosophy" by many of our early chiropractic pioneers. Like our medical colleague Andrew Weil, MD and others that have espoused the wellness concepts, they cannot undo their education foundation and orientation. Instead they restructure their footing to allow a more flexible medical foundation that can encompass a wellness and prevention integrative approach to health care.

My Cherokee grandmother influenced my start as a Chiropractor because she taught in my early childhood what nature could offer if one understood the underpinnings of mother earth. But not everyone was as fortunate as me in having a grandmother that understood nature and how important it is to have a foundation and lifestyle based in health and wellness from their very childhood.

No single specialty has the corner on health, wellness and longevity. All specialty practices work for different people at different times and not others. This is why Chinese Medicine, Ayurvedic and Asian traditional practices as well as, Chiropractic, Osteopathic and Homeopathy have worked and are still working to help people regardless of all the scientific reasoning to the contrary. Modern conventional medicine is beyond a doubt as good or better than anything that can be provided for acute illness and injury, but for health, wellness and chronic conditions alternative practices have much to offer.

PREVENTION

We must all come together at this stage and time and let our specialties work toward health and wellness of the human population. We can see from the past that even as good, and in some cases miraculous, as modern pharmaceutical and technological based medicine has become it is too cumbrous and expensive for all but the wealthiest. Even our modern western society cannot afford the expense it is costing to fight disease. Keeping healthy and understanding prevention - the lifestyle that keeps a person on the wellness continuum and is what we as humans are trying to achieve.

There is no doubt the healthcare system in America has experienced unparalleled changes in the past decade and will face even more in the next decades. The enormous explosion in communication and information technology, the American people demand more and faster service to be fully available in one location. Today's society expects instant gratification from top experts in the field in an affordable, convenient location.

All this is not saying there won't be challenges with new products, treatments, equipment and services that are constantly changing. Some of these are completely revolutionizing the way practice is being done. This is part of the excitement and challenge of being part of the transformation of medicine and how it will be practiced. For instance, Brown University and the Rhode Island Hospital System are among the innovators of the wellness and prevention professional push. The College of Women and Children has in place a wellness and prevention program to teach the staff and the patients new concepts that can be utilized in nutrition, exercise and other alternative strategies that have not been made available in conventional medicine before. This new generation of health care professional will see the big merge (Integrative Medicine) of the practice philosophies for the betterment of patient centered health and wellness care.

What to Expect in a Typical Clinical Appearance

Let's begin with the most important part of any team, the front line. The front office staff begins with a receptionist, who is the first impression the patient gets of a medical office or clinic. The person in this position will need to be courteous, friendly and an exceptional advocate for the patient, remember they are the first impression of the office. This individual is responsible for receiving and booking new patients, making appointments, account charges for each patient, and answering general questions about office details. Some questions about insurance can be answered by the receptionist but may have to involve the office manager as well as the administrator. Many clinics get so busy with patient care that insurance coverage becomes a totally new job description.

It is at this point you may see a change in the front office staff of an IM office or clinic compared with the typical medical, osteopathic or chiropractic office that you would see anywhere in America. This is because of insurance coverage and laws. There are few insurance companies that cover prevention, wellness or functional procedures even if done by a medical practitioner. Offices today have become more innovative and creative in their coverage of preventive, wellness and rehabilitative services performed. More offices are going back to the cash type practice and shifting the insurance coverage responsibility back to the patient and the insurance company getting the doctor out of the picture except for providing a diagnosis and treatment description.

Clinical Needs for an Integrative Medicine Practice

You may find as many as four or five practitioners working together. Some offices have them together like a single staff and other clinics have them in separate areas of the building completely independent. This all depends on the size of the clinical staff that is required to do the job efficiently and how your state laws are written. The practitioner of Integrative Medicine and Wellness needs to meet a few basic requirements that are accepted by the National Integrative Medicine Association as standards of care.

The clinic or office needs to have a clinical staff of several specialty practitioners or if it is a single practitioner they need to be certified in several different fields. There are Medical Doctors (MD), Osteopaths (DO), Chiropractors (DC), Acupuncturist (DOM), Naturopathy Doctor (ND), and other specialties such as Nurse Practitioners that now do a lot more than they did a decade ago in preventive care procedures. The safest thing for the consumer to do is check the credentials of the practitioner. There are states with very strict laws regarding a practitioner using a specialty name and other states that have very loose regulations.

Keep in mind who and what you are looking for with an Integrative practitioner or an Integrative Clinic. There should be a choice of practice philosophies about wellness and prevention regardless of the degree of the practitioner. In other words, you can begin with an MD for part of your care because they are your family physician and should know your likes and desires of your health and preventive care. Talk to your GP about referral to a practitioner such as: a DC or DO for another more musculoskeletal oriented aspect of your wellness care. You might want to see a Nutritionist for nutritional advice or a Psychologist for emotional health consultation. Many times they are not in the same office simply because practice philosophies have not progressed far enough or there may not be physical room for the practices to merge. You may find any of the following professionals sitting in an Integrative practice situation either alone or in a group.

The **Medical Director** is a role in the new practice model involving leadership and cooperation with the other professions dealing with the problems of today's health care. The Medical Director could be an MD, a PhD (such as in Medical Administration) or an EdD (Education Doctorate) or one of the other specialties covered below. There are some state laws that prevent the direction or supervision of some doctors by other doctors so this will make a difference in some states. The essential thing is the Director must know and understand both Integrative and Alternative Medicine practice methods as well as conventional medicine.

The Medical Director in an integrative practice knows and understands that prevention and wellness come first. Then if it fails to correct the problem or condition you go the next stage of defense, pharmaceuticals. If they don't do the job, that's when it's time to look to more radical means. For too many years it was pharmacy first and then surgery without much hesitation. Our research has followed this for over fifty years and found this is not always the best methodology to use. A problem should be approached from the most conservative means first before going on to a more radical method that is often more expensive and time consuming. This is why today you will find more and more of your Family, General Practitioners and Internists who are more understanding of the desire to try a more conservative method first, rather than going to pharmaceuticals first. The Medical Director acts as a gatekeeper and must be educated in the conservative and the radical side of medicine in order to properly guide the patient to the best result for their problem.

The **Osteopath** or Doctor of Osteopathic Medicine is a medical doctor who has also been trained with the underlying philosophy that the body has a natural tendency to heal itself but this can be disrupted by imbalances in the musculoskeletal system.

The Osteopath and wellness go together like hand and glove if you follow the original tenants of the profession. Andrew Still, father of Osteopathy, felt that the body at times needed a little help from the biochemical world to spur it back to normal when it was too far from health. Many in the Osteopathic profession have become dominated by the pharmaceutical industry and have lost the foundation principles of the profession of prevention first by living a healthy life to maintain wellness.

The **Chiropractor** or Doctor of Chiropractic (DC) you may find to be the most open to prevention, integrative and wellness procedures because this is the Chiropractic profession's foundation. Some Doctors of Chiropractic may choose to practice within a very narrow scope of Chiropractic philosophy and just correct the subluxations or misalignments of the spine. Others may choose to practice the full scope of their education and philosophy and include exercise, physical therapy, laser therapy, nutritional analysis, ultrasound, electrical stimulation, and treatment of lacerations, strains and sprains as well as emotional problems.

This is one reason why the Chiropractic profession has been so successful in practice, because they look for the cause of a condition or problem rather than just cover the symptoms with a prescription. Then the attempt at correction is the treatment approach they choose within their arsenal of methods to correct the problem. In most Integrative practices you will find the services of a Chiropractor available in the office or very close by for referral purposes.

The **Acupuncturist**. Many people have been to a Chiropractor and not found relief for one reason or the other. Acupuncture is another treatment alternative and can help with a wide array of problems including headaches, neck pain, low back pain, nausea and fatigue. Some people cannot accept the feeling of their bones being manipulated and decide they want acupuncture instead. While many people do not know and understand the Yin/Yang basis of the energies of acupuncture, most know it is one of the most well-known practices in the world for pain. This we want to cover in more detail a little later. For now let's just say the acupuncturist treats on a more functional basis for your problems. This will be explained in greater measure in more detail a little later in our presentation.

Another valuable asset to a wellness team is a **Massage Therapist**. They may have been educated in the local community college or at a private school of bodywork. They must possess state and local credentials that they are certified in their profession and field of expertise. The requirements may differ in many states and you will have to check with the Massage Therapy Board of Examiners to check credentials further.

These types of practitioners are the essential elements of an Integrative practice. They can be mixed and matched anyway that the Medical Director wishes. This method is how many have combined the alternatives and allowed complimentary health care to develop into a specific practice over the past 30 years in the form of Integrative Medicine geared toward prevention and wellness of the individual.

The benefits of the team approach to patient care have many leading hospitals, research and education centers embracing integrative care. These include MD Anderson in Houston; Moffitt Cancer in Tampa; and the University of Miami, as well as a number of other leading hospitals and medical education centers like Johns Hopkins.

Chapter IV

CHIROPRACTIC

John L. Stump, DC, PhD, EdD

"Man is what he believes."

ANTON CHEKHOV (1860-1904)

A BRIEF HISTORY

I was introduced to Chiropractic early in my life. During my sophomore year of high school, while playing volleyball I jumped up to spike a shot and twisted the wrong way. I felt an electric shock down the arm and then numbness. Our physical education teacher immediately took me down to the school nurse, they consulted with the principal and soon I was in the coach's car heading to a doctor.

Our high school was in a rural community called Denton, Maryland with no hospital within 20 miles, but there were two or three doctors in town. We pulled up to a big white house and walked into the entrance. We were greeted by a nice lady who asked a number of questions about my problem and how I got hurt. Then we were asked to sit in the waiting area. After a short time, I was escorted to a room in the back, marked clinic and asked to sit on the table. In a few minutes a tall, slender, dark haired man with a moustache, like Clark Gable greeted me with "Hi John, what have you done now." I didn't know how he knew me, especially how he said, "what have you done now." It was true I was no angel in high school, even though my mother called me Johnny Angel. I replied “This wasn’t my fault. I was in physical education class and jumped up to spike a ball when a hot pain shot down my arm from my neck, then my arm became numb.”

He asked if this was the first time it had ever happened and did I have any other physical problems, as he led me to a special table in another room.

“Yes, this is the first time and I hope the last this happens, I have no other problems.”

He asked if I would take my shirt off and lie on my stomach. He began probing my neck. On the right side it felt normal but on the left there was pain in certain spots and I told him. He asked me to turn over and again he began probing the muscles.

He began to explain what was wrong while he was moving my neck in different directions. "Your neck went one way and your arm and body went another during that spike of the volleyball. You caused a minor 'whiplash' in your neck.

We call this a subluxation, when the muscles hold vertebrae out of its normal position and it causes pain in the area when the nerve and muscle is stretched and strained."

In a few minutes he stopped the motion and with a sudden snap of his hands there was movement and a “pop” in my neck. Within a matter of minutes there was relief of the pain and most of the numbness. Of course my first question was, “can I dress out to play football this afternoon.” I lived for football. My dad and I just had a disagreement that morning at breakfast about how he would prefer me to play baseball because football was so violent! “No, you can’t dress-out today, but after I see you tomorrow it may be possible,” the Doc said.

As we were leaving I noticed a sign on the door that read: Dr. Gordon Wheat, D.C. *Chiropractor* had been under his name. When we returned to school I was feeling so much better, but they wouldn’t allow me to go to class, only sit in the library. I decided to look up the words *Chiropractor* and *Chiropractic*. In reading the definitions, I found that manipulation of the spine usually done by hand to correct a subluxation was the real essence. There was an explanation of the “tor” at the end of the word, as in ‘Chiropractor’ meaning one who does the manipulation. With “tic” at the end of the word it designates the profession of Chiropractic.

Yes, that was what Dr. Wheat explained to me in his office that day. Now here it is 50 years later and the interpretation is still not clear to many people outside of the healing arts as to who Chiropractors are and what Chiropractic does. That is part of the reason for writing this book. We want everyone to know and understand the procedures that are used in Chiropractic as well as all the other alternative practices.

Musculoskeletal System

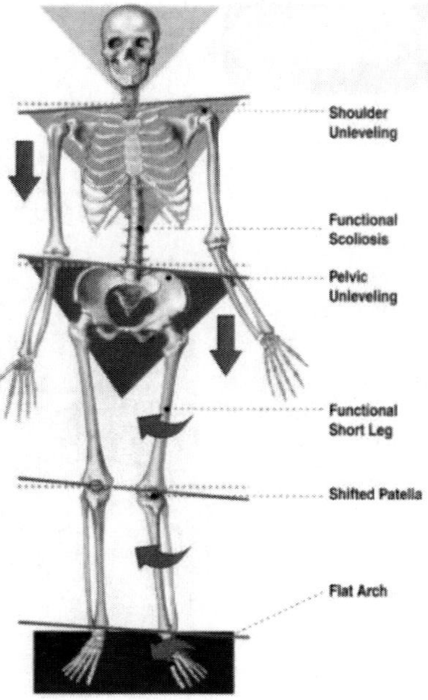

Chiropractors deal with the Neuro-musculoskeletal system most of the time. However, they recognize the fact they are treating a whole person and you can't separate out the body's systems as is done in an anatomy textbook. In reality the body's systems do not operate independently of each other. They interact in a myriad of ways. Since this is the case, the Chiropractor is responsible for much more than the Neuro-musculoskeletal system examining, diagnosing, and treating patients.

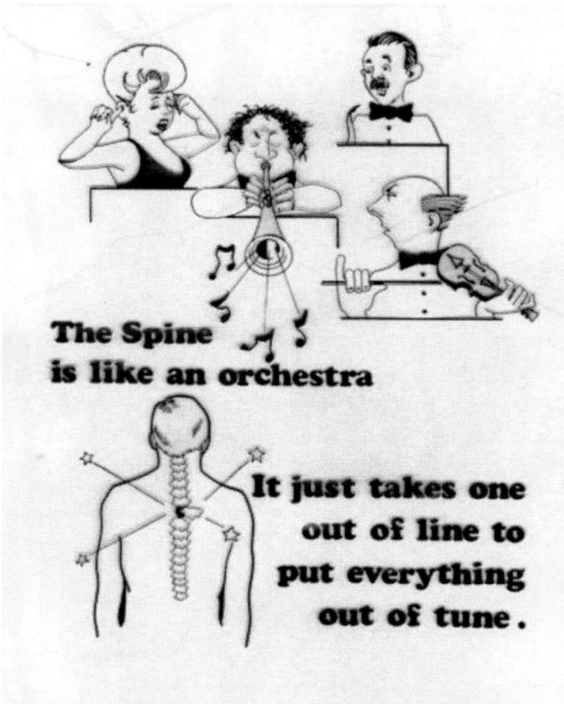

Figure 2. An Illustration indicating the importance of a single motor unit.

It is impossible to separate the physiological function and the anatomical structure of the vertebral motor unit the Chiropractor is responsible to correct. The nervous system is housed within the motor unit of the spine and the nerves travel to every part of human anatomy. For this reason Chiropractors finds themselves not only working with the neuromuscular but with the psychological, digestive, endocrine, and the other systems simply because the nervous system coordinates and controls most of the bodily functions. As a result, anything that interferes with the communication from the brain and nervous system to a particular body structure is a part of the responsibility of the Chiropractic Physician to help correct.

Another reason Chiropractors as integrative physicians are securitizing values and outcomes of the studies that are being collected by the Central Illinois Neuroscience Foundation (CINF), of Bloomington, IL. (ACA news April 2014 www.acatoday.org) This not-for profit organization was established in 1996 for the purpose of enhancing neurological health care through education and research.

Integrative Setting

Dr. Steve Troyanovich, Chiropractor and Research Committee Chairman for the Central Illinois Neuroscience Foundation, has been a leader in establishing this new integrative position for the Chiropractic profession. Chiropractic's established emphasis on research and education in this integrative setting has opened a new avenue of regard and clarification for the profession. These Neuro-specialities working together have helped demonstrate that Chiropractic is not merely a musculoskeletal science but a neuromusculoskeletal practice that considers the holistic aspects of the human.

In addition, the University of Bridgeport in Connecticut has now established a concentration in Neuromusculoskeletal Medicine especially for Chiropractors and allied branches of the healing arts designed to meet the needs of the modern Chiropractic physician. Many Chiropractic colleges are now advancing the "University Concept" of education that has expanded and embraced much more in the allied and complimentary fields of the healing arts.

About Lower Back Pain

This is one of the most researched and common problems in modern man. It spurred an entire profession and now nearly 70% of the human population will at some time suffer the condition to some degree. In fact, the North American Spine Society reports that studies have shown the cost of all spine care in the United States is estimated to exceed 100 billion dollars. This is just about equivalent to the cost of all cancer care in the United States. A word of advice for the four-fifths of Americans that know back pain: Consider everything before surgery even if it seems extreme to the patient. Those who jump on the medical merry-go-round of prescription, MRI, more imaging, epidural injections, and being passed from one specialist to another until eventually surgery.

The Chiropractic profession has said for at least the last four decades that more than ninety percent (90%) of back problems can be resolved with simple, non-invasive procedures that the chiropractic profession has taught for eras. Yes, they involve bone, muscle and nerve repositioning but that's what happens during most injuries. The injury has caused a mechanical alteration of "normal" position, which at times is micro and others is macro. This is where the art of Chiropractic is applied to attempt to correct the subluxation and thus mitigate the patient's pain. Yes, the individual may want some anti-inflammatory drug (NSAID) such as ibuprofen (Motrin, Advil) or naproxen (Aleve) to ease the pain while working the problem out and that's not a problem as long as it is short term (less than 2 weeks). Taking these medications long term (more than 4 weeks) may lead to gastrointestinal problems and you will have to consult your family physician or internist about the medication.

Remember Chiropractors are the highest rated healthcare practitioners for low- back pain treatments – treating over 27 million Americans annually – more than physical therapist, pain management specialist, orthopedist, neurologist, and neurosurgeons. Even more than primary care physicians like your family medicine or internist according to a study done by the Washington State Department of Labor and Industry in 2013. This is not surprising noted Dr. Hamm, one of the authors of the study, when you consider that injured workers are 28 *less likely* to undergo spinal surgery if their first point of contact is a Chiropractor rather than an orthopedist, and that treatment for lower-back pain will cost up to twenty-five percent less than treatment started by the MD. (Keeney et al., 2013)

Just remember always try the most conservative treatment first before going to more radical means regardless of your insurance coverage.

FUTURE WITH CHIROPRACTIC

More than one hundred years after the discovery and development of the science, philosophy and art of Chiropractic, it is still evolving just as other dynamic skill in the medical field. No longer is it necessary and in some cases important that the subluxation be corrected by hand. Now there are other means of manipulation that may at times be more suitable. Much like the surgeon's job no longer requires doing everything by hand. They now have the option of robotics and mechanical means that may be more precise than human hands, and allow performing tasks once thought impossible by the surgical profession.

D.D. Palmer the founder of Chiropractic and B.J. his son, who further advanced and developed it, would marvel at the many changes and advances in the profession since 1895. As they stood over looking Davenport, Iowa in their building on Brady Hill they obviously knew they had a great discovery in their "hands." Today there are nearly 100,000 Chiropractors in the United States and thousands more around the world in every modern nation on earth.

At this point in our discussion of Chiropractic we have to decide if it is important to dig a little deeper and shed light upon some of the new discoveries in the Chiropractic profession. The subluxation may be either: physical, emotion, or chemical in nature and often all three together... remember 'holism' is reality.

- Physical: In that these may be due to trauma, repetitive motion or in many cases a lack of motion. As an example a fall, motor vehicle accident, sports injury, at work in lifting, pushing or pulling can cause a stress, strain and/or subluxation to manifest.
- Emotional/and or mental: These problems develop as the result of stress from grief, anger, fear, etc., the muscles react in ways that can cause a subluxation or nerve irritation to develop in the nervous system.
- Chemical: Today there are literally thousands of chemicals that are harmful to the body and cause a toxic reaction when exposed to them. This is may be from certain foods, drinks, tobacco, drugs and or environmental pollutants. Causing the nervous system to react and create a neurological and often pathological reaction to occur.

Neurological Responses

Most people do not even know when they develop a neurological response because the subluxation has not caused pain, signs or symptoms yet. Many scientific investigators call this a silent stealth because it will cause deterioration in function of the nervous system to begin even before the symptoms appear. This is why people can often not understand why they felt so well yet had a heart attack, stroke or other incident like cancer only a short time later. This is why the modern DC or Doctor of Chiropractic does a very thorough examination and diagnostic work up, which may include lab tests, MRI, CT or other imaging necessary before initiating treatment.

APPLIED KINESIOLOGY (AK)

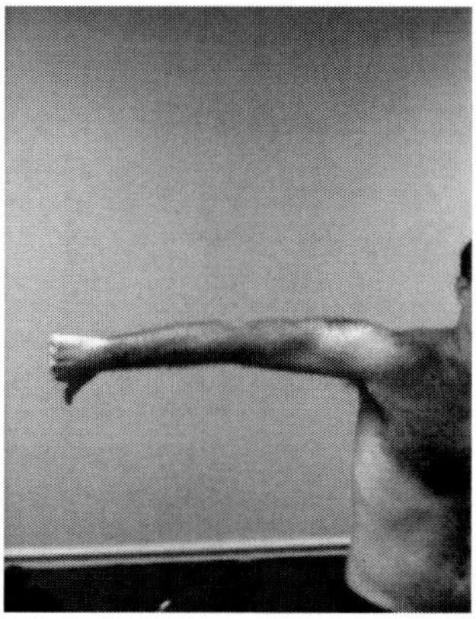

One of the advanced techniques and procedures discovered and developed over the many years of growth in the Chiropractic profession is Applied Kinesiology (AK). George Goodheart, DC, developed it in his clinic in Dearborn, Michigan over fifty years ago. Dr. Goodheart saw that Chiropractic was more than just "structural" in its analysis, correction and rehabilitation. It takes into account not just bones, but also nerves and muscles. He realized there was something more transpiring in the treatment than could meet the eye. Dr. Goodheart began to read and talk to experts in the field of Oriental Medicine about what was known as "Qi" (pronounced "chee"), an unseen energy system in and around the human body. The more he studied the more he saw this system helped explain why he was getting some of the amazing results he had seen in his clinical evaluations and investigations.

Today Applied Kinesiology is an established technique that can be utilized by any professional willing to take the time to learn the western and eastern concepts that bridge the two systems and create a dynamic muscle testing and balancing procedure. AK has become a diagnostic and analytical procedure. Much could be elaborated on about the techniques in this system of correction procedures but suffice it to say that Applied Kinesiology is only in the infant stages of development. For further details refer to a new complete system of AK textbooks being published by the International College of Applied Kinesiology (ICAK) led by author and publisher Dr. Scott Cuthbert. *Applied Kinesiology Essentials: The Missing Link* is just one of a three book series.

There are thousands of AK practitioners around the world now that the system is over fifty years old, with every professional specialty utilizing different aspects of the system for their specialty in medicine. General Practitioners and Family Physicians of rural and impoverished nations are now using AK as a quick and simple diagnostic method that can be used in place of imaging procedures when they are not available. Dentist, Podiatrist, Acupuncturist and other specialist like Physical Therapist have found the system beneficial to their area of medicine and health care.

The nervous and meridian system work together and can both be analyzed by the method we introduced earlier called Applied Kinesiology (AK) that brings the principles of Eastern and Western health care together. The meridian system will be explained in more detail in the Acupuncture chapter.

AK utilizes the teachings of Acupuncture, Chiropractic, Nutrition and a number of other important biomechanical and physiological principles that are used in physical medicine and integrative wellness procedures such as muscle testing to achieve balancing and correcting the individual's problem. Muscle testing as used in AK is applied Oriental Medicine principles.

TECHNIQUES AND METHODOLOGY

In the Chiropractic profession there are hundreds of treatment techniques when you count and variations of the original techniques developed by the early Chiropractic pioneers. These initial techniques were all to pursue the analysis and correction of subluxations in the human body. Here I must digress to say a subluxation can be present in any vertebrate organism not just the human. The specialty of Veterinary Chiropractic has developed in the past 40 years. As a matter of fact, I was involved in starting the first Veterinary Chiropractic organization. This was at Palmer College of Chiropractic in Davenport, Iowa in 1975. While at Palmer College I was honored to serve as the first President of the Veterinary Chiropractic organization until my graduation in the fall 1976.

The primary objective in all techniques and procedures of Chiropractic is to detect and use the juxtaposition and correct the subluxation regardless of where it is found in the body. Some techniques may be better for the correction of one type over the other and are preferred by the patient or the practitioner. It is most important to find the technique system best for practitioner and patient and incorporate it into the health and wellness care strategy.

THERAPY IN CHIROPRACTIC

Many people can't understand the difference in Chiropractic from office to office. Let us shed a little light on this mystery. When D.D. Palmer developed Chiropractic in 1895, there was only emphasis on correction of the subluxation. Then some practitioners started using whatever technique modalities would help the patient, such as applying heat, cold, etc. As a result there was a schism in the profession between the purists and the mixers. The purists felt there was no need for anything other than the Chiropractic adjustment (manipulation) to help the patient. However, the mixers felt that a better result was achieved by using heat or cold to relax the muscle prior to the adjustment. This philosophy is still continuing one hundred years later in the Chiropractic profession. You will find those who only adjust the two or three top vertebrae and never do anything else to the body until the next checkup. Yet, down the street you may find another DC who uses everything legal within the profession to help correct the subluxation and help the patient with pain.

This difference in practice philosophy is good for the profession according to many experts in the healing arts. It's like having the democrats and the republicans in the same profession. One thing it has done is expand the horizons of the Chiropractic profession being able to use the many modalities available.

A good case in point is the recent advent of the low level laser sometimes called the cold laser. The laser (light energy) seemed like something out of a *Star Wars* movie with light sabers. Today, Low Level Laser Therapy (LLLT) is used in nearly every sports medicine event and in many conservative injury management cases of strains, sprains and other conditions like fibromyalgia, neuropathy, osteoarthritis and carpal tunnel syndrome to name a few. A study published in 2013 by the Public Library of Science stated, "One area that is attracting growing interest in this scope is the use of Transcranial LLLT to treat stroke and traumatic brain injury (TBI)." This was again confirmed by the Wellman Center for Photo Medicine at Massachusetts General Hospital, which works in collaboration with Harvard Medical School. Among their many research initiatives, LLLT for traumatic brain injury is among the top areas being investigated.

If the Chiropractic profession had continued in their narrow scope of practice breakthroughs such as this with LLLT may have gone undiscovered for many years.

There are many other therapies used now in Chiropractic practice. Individual Chiropractors will chose which therapies they use depending on their philosophy of treatment.

As the American Chiropractic Association website states:

> "As evidence supporting the effectiveness of Chiropractic continues to emerge with new research, health care consumers are turning in large numbers to Chiropractic care – a form of health care aimed at primarily at enhancing a patient's overall health and well-being without drugs or surgery. More than 25 million people each year visit the Chiropractor for a variety of conditions, and more and more medical referrals are being made each year."

Chapter V

ACUPUNCTURE/ ORIENTAL MEDICINE/ CHINESE MEDICINE

John L. Stump, DC, PhD, EdD

"The thought manifests as the word. The word manifests as the deed. The deed develops into habit. And the habit hardens into character. So watch the thought and its ways with care. And let it spring from love, born out of concern for all beings."

BUDDHA (C. 563-c. 483 BC)

HUANG TI, THE YELLOW EMPEROR

THE YIN AND YANG

Let us begin this study with a very foreign concept of "Qi." Human life is the life process activated and maintained by what Oriental Medicine describes as "vital energy," "life force," or "Qi" as it is known in the East. The main supply of this energy is derived first from genetics and then from the environment through such processes as:

1. Respiration
2. Nutrition

It is converted into assailable form by certain organs and is stored by the body and distributed throughout the system by other organs. In Oriental Medicine it is a basic premise that this vital energy (or life force) is a manifestation of a monistic unitary bipolar energy (one energy divided into two equal but opposite forces), which in living organisms, permeates every cell and tissue of the organism in form, structure and function. These equal but opposite forces are what are known as Yin and Yang. They are not opposite in the sense of fighting each other, but rather complementary opposites that together achieve balance.

In the East, Yin and Yang are involved in the conception of how the universe started. This is exemplified by the fact that Yang represents birth and Yin represents death. Between the two extremes of birth and death, there occurs some type of continuum, or series of rhythms, balances, tensions, relaxations and cycles of predominance of Yang or Yin energy. The totality in any organism represents its life span, sickness and wellness both being part of the continuum of life.

Acupuncture is a therapeutic approach for balancing the flow and distribution of Qi or energy in the body. This method has been used in Asia for thousands of years. A report in *Science* (1992) stated that the mummified remains of a man thought to be over 5,000 years old were found to have corresponding tattoos where acupuncture points are located. This evidence suggests that a form of acupuncture may have been practiced in Eurasia more than 2000 years earlier than previously speculated. (Dorter et al., 1999)

This branch of the healing arts is the most ancient of all the branches and probably the most challenging for the Western mind to understand. During the first year of the four-year pursuit of my Chiropractic degree I became interested in President Nixon's trip to China, but not for political reasons. Mine where for health reasons. It was 1971 and James Reston had accompanied Nixon's Whitehouse staff to China. Reston was invited to view the procedures of a healing art little know in the west at that time... that of acupuncture.

Reston on his second day in China experienced unexplained lower abdominal pain. He told his interpreter and they immediately arranged for him to be taken to a nearby hospital that served the diplomatic corps in Peking (now called Beijing). After a thorough examination by a top MD by the name of Professor Wu Wei-jan, Reston was diagnosed with appendicitis and immediate surgery was recommended. He agreed and was taken to surgery where they injected him with Xylocain and Benzocaine, which anesthetized the area and the entire procedure took less than 20 minutes to successfully perform. However, on the second day Reston developed a sharp pain in the same general area. The hospital brought acupuncturist Li Chang-Yuan to attend to his pain. After Reston's approval, three needles were applied to the outside of his arms at about the elbows and below the knees. These locations correspond to intestine stimulation points. Then a procedure called 'Ai' (Moxibustion, which involves the use of dried mugwort) was used near his abdomen for a few minutes. Reston said, "It looked like a stump of a cheap cigar was being burned next my abdomen." Within the hour the pain mysteriously disappeared never to return again. From that time on Reston wanted to be sure the information became known to the English-speaking world and he wrote his famous article that put acupuncture in the media headlines in America.

During my Chiropractic training I had become friends with a young Japanese student from Kobe, Japan by the name of Shingo Fukinbara. He had been an author, gymnast and a black belt. Had graduated from Acupuncture school, spoke three languages and was a teacher of an ancient philosophy, all before he was twenty-five. When asked why he came to America to study Chiropractic he would state, "The philosophy of Yin/Yang explains it best. Acupuncture's healing energy is yin and Chiropractic's healing energy is yang. Together they can attain the majority of health goals one needs for wellness, health and life. If you were to be a practitioner such as me it would be most beneficial to your practice in ways beyond comprehension."

Dr. Fukinbara stated, "When one begins the study of Oriental Medicine, it is with the utmost importance to realize that the orientation is quite different from the present western medical approach. Though Western medical knowledge may be an advantage in some respects, it also may be a disadvantage in others."

The more I studied the human structure and physiology the more I found he was correct in his analysis of the function of Chiropractic and Acupuncture. In Chiropractic school we talked of prevention and preventive care, wellness and trying to get the patient to present before a problem induced an office visit. About ten percent would think on a "preventive basis" for their care. However, the clear majority was reactionary to their pain level. Meaning they would only come in when the pain was so bad they could do nothing else but see a doctor. Then the patient would stop treatment as soon as they were out of pain.

This became the norm all the way through my four years of Chiropractic education. When my graduation date approached the plan was to move to the Delmarva Peninsula (Delaware, Maryland and Virginia) and begin practice. But my friend and martial arts teacher in Iowa, Dr. Shingo Fukinbara, asked if I had considered going on to get my advanced credentials in Oriental Medicine, especially acupuncture. It was not a consideration on my radar at that time due to finances and family time. When he explained to me about a post-graduate scholarship, that caught my attention.

To make a long story short, my plans changed and my compass was reset toward Japan for the fall of the following year to enroll in a post-doctoral acupuncture program. My Japanese up to that point consisted of four years of translations between Dr. Fukinbara and the English he should be writing and speaking during the classes and the martial arts he was teaching. I had to reverse my thought process and plug in Japanese as my main language and English as my second. It took me awhile but after a few months I was on my way with acupuncture study during the day and the martial art of Shorinji Kempo at night. I was told this was the immersion method of learning a language or like my Dad used to say, "Sink or Swim time."

I'm not going to bore you with the trials and tribulations of the differences in the life style changes necessary; diet, language, thinking and mannerisms of living in Japan as compared to America. The one thing that remained the same was the fact that when a person was in pain a doctor was sought. In Japan, it was not the MD first, but the acupuncturist was the 'go to person' to alleviate pain. As my acupuncture education progressed and my scope increased, my knowledge was tested with every clinical case seen. I ended up seeing thousands over the years in Japan.

After my second year, because I already had a B.S. and doctoral degree in Chiropractic, plus being a foreigner, my curriculum changed to a clinical format. My doctoral committee allowed me a great deal of latitude in my studies. They asked if travel to China to study at Shaanxi University Hospital with the college of Traditional Chinese Medicine could be in my plan. My interest in China was high anyway, so I bit the bullet financially and took the leap of faith needed at the time.

After three months in Shaanxi China, at one of the largest hospitals, accommodating 5,000 patients each day, I was directed to other clinics in China. Then on to South Korea, Philippines, Thailand and even a hospital in

Turkey where one of the hospital's top acupuncturists had graduated from Shaanxi. After working in all these countries, I found that pain was the main factor involved in the majority of cases, regardless of locale. I saw many other cases but pain cases were the clear majority from one end of Asia to the other.

After my acupuncture education was completed I returned to the United States in the wake of a new development in health care... Acupuncture was making news headlines!

THE DIAGNOSIS IN CHINESE MEDICINE

Throughout history, doctors and practitioners have used physical observation to monitor the health and wellness status of their family, friends and others. The preliminary physical examination the western healing arts use today is a prime example of this. The doctor will take the blood pressure and listen to the heart through a stethoscope to assess the patient's heart health. He shines a light into each eye to see if pupils respond normally, a remarkably simple test for healthy adrenal function. He then looks through the iris with an ophthalmoscope to examine the retina at the back of the eye and hitting your knee with a little triangle hammer may check your reflexes. The patient is asked to stick out his tongue. Using a tongue depressor the practitioner moves the tongue aside enabling him to observe the throat and tonsils, to examine their color, looking for signs of inflammation and infection.

The purpose of all this: he is looking for evidence of abnormalities associated with an illness or disease process. This is a standard preliminary examination today by western standards, but in no way as thorough as it could be.

Historically, before the era of modern medicine, the practitioner observed, smelled and even at times tasted the patient's urine to check for conditions like diabetes. In an age-old test for scurvy in children, a prevalent disease before its cause was known, the practitioner would ask the parent to hold the child up by the ankles and shake them. The physician was listening for the rattle of bone on bone. The rattle indicated the probable loss of connective tissue and possible presence of scurvy. This was of course long before the introduction of sophisticated and technological diagnostic methods of today.

The diagnostic methods of the west are to find and get rid of disease. Whereas the eastern practitioner had a more inclusive approach as I learned from my education in Oriental Medicine in both Japan and China. For instance, the practitioner of western medicine has not been trained to check the tongue's coating and look for abnormalities in the size, shape, color, and for markings and fissures. The western practice of shoving aside the tongue misses the opportunities to check for nutritional deficiencies and disease processes that may be displayed in the tongue.

There are many such examples of pathological changes that can be detected from straightforward observations by a trained practitioner. In addition to the tongue, observing physical changes in the fingernails, eyes, skin, and hair may reveal deficiencies and abnormal conditions. By utilizing physical observation the good diagnostician can see conditions and deficiencies before they begin. This knowledge enables an individual and the practitioner to be more precise in the care of the organs tissues and systems of the body.

There are many diagnostic methods in Oriental Medicine but this text does not attempt to explain or go into the depths of Chinese diagnostics but suffice it to say the western practitioner could learn a great deal by pulling from some the eastern diagnostic methodology.

Pain

All the teaching though my chiropractic and acupuncture education emphasized prevention and wellness, although what really brought the patient to your clinic was pain. In retrospect the Chinese were correct in their teaching, "You must get the patient out of pain first," was their doctrine and pain is very different for everyone.

Patients present in different states of pain. Some don't even know they have measurable pain and others think the pain they have is beyond measure.

This is why chiropractic and acupuncture work so well together. Some people you can't touch to manipulate, these patients are called very yin and can't tolerate the sound of the manipulation (which is yang). Others can't stand the thought of a prick of a pin, these are called very yang. Usually, this is when 'what method to use' with the patient to sooth their mind and repair their body the fastest, quizzes the experience and education of the doctor.

This is when the analogy of a toolbox is beneficial to explain the needs of the practitioner. When you first graduate from a professional healing arts school the professors always say, "Now that you have the tools, go out and heal those in need." However, you only know what they have taught you. You don't realize you are limited in the job according to the tools you have and the education to administer those tools.

Let me explain. Most patients see a chiropractor for lower back pain, neck pain or headache pain. These are the three most common problems seen by a Chiropractor. It just so happens that the new wave of interest in acupuncture was because of the same thing… pain. The previously described acupuncture experience of James Reston in China opened a whole new avenue for all doctors working with pain patients. This also ushered in a new profession (Acupuncture/Chinese Medicine/Oriental Medicine) onto the medical stage with the limelight beaming on the result of its performance. So far, the result has been as bright as the spotlight was thought to be even without complete scientific explanation for the past nearly 50 years of my involvement.

Proactive Approach to Pain

Many Americans suffer from long term or what's known as chronic pain. In fact, according to the National Centers for Health Statistics, more than one quarter of Americans (26%) age twenty and over, an estimated 76.5 million people report they experience chronic pain. They get up in the morning in pain and go to bed in the evening without relief of the pain. Most have to get up during the night due to the pain. Such pain restricts activities and limits lifestyle choices.

Both Chiropractic and Acupuncture seek to help the body function at its most optimal level via the correction of pain causing imbalances. In order to understand how both Chiropractic and Acupuncture can help chronic pain sufferers, let's look at the definition of pain.

Pain is not a bad entity in and of itself. Of course for those experiencing it, there is no enjoyment involved. By looking at the whole picture you can see that pain is the body's manner of sending an ALARM to the body. The message is that something is incorrect and off balance in the body and can't be ignored any longer.

Pain that comes on quickly and lasts a relatively short period of time is defined as acute pain. If a person feels a sufficient amount of discomfort, they will stop doing the activity that was occurring at the time of pain. This is a protective mechanism constructed into the body's nervous system to help prevent additional injury. It is the body's response to injury. For instance if you twist an ankle while jogging, the pain you feel is acute pain. In this manner pain can be useful as long as it is controlling excessive activity and helping to keep us healthy. However, pain can get out of control and continue long after its usefulness has been achieved. Chronic pain is pain that persists far beyond the normal time period to heal the sprain or strain of the ankle

Chronic Pain

Chronic pain has many sources:

- Injuries that did not heal correctly or completely
- Long-term disease
- Acquired disability pain
- Scar tissue

Of course, there are other sources, but regardless of the cause of chronic pain it encompasses an unsolved concern with the body. The issue with chronic pain is it starts a vicious cycle in the body that leads to more pain. The longer we feel the pain, the more our body tries to accommodate the pain. This is often through unusual body movements and posture, and through a reduction of activities. The more the body accommodates the pain, the more difficult it is to get rid of it on a permanent basis as a result this cycle becomes very hard to break.

This is where Integrative Medicine begins to play a part in the health care of an individual. Scientific principles state that although injury or illness may be the original cause of pain, everything that happens to the body involves the brain and nervous system and everything that involves the nervous system causes a reaction in the Meridian System that is explained in acupuncture and Oriental Medicine.

Meridian System

Usually, only those familiar with acupuncture and Oriental Medicine understand the Meridian System and its function in the body. Here is an explanation of the Meridian System.

There are 14 main meridians in Acupuncture (Deadman, 2001). The Chinese believe these meridians carry life force (Mayor and Micozzi, 2011). There are 12 called the "primary medians" which are bilateral, meaning they affect both the right and left sides of the body. These primary meridians are associated with specific organs and/or glandular functions and include lung, large intestine, heart, small intestine, pericardium (the sac around the heart), triple warmer, liver, gall bladder, spleen and stomach. The "triple warmer" is also called the "triple burner" and is a bit different from the others in that it doesn't deal with a specific organ. The "triple" part of the name refers to the upper, mid, and lower parts of the body, and this meridian deals with the flow of energy among these areas.

SUMMARY OF THE TWELVE PRIMARY MERIDIANS

12 Meridians	Acupuncture Location
Heart	Inside front of arm
Small Intestine	Inside back of arm
Bladder	Outside back of leg
Kidney	Inside front of leg
Pericardium	Middle front of arm
Triple Warmer	Middle back of arm
Gall Bladder	Middle back of leg
Liver	Middle front of leg
Lung	Outside front of arm
Large Intestine	Inside back of arm
Stomach	Inside front of leg
Spleen	Outside front of leg

The Gall Bladder meridian is illustrated as an example of the meridian energy flow in the body, remember there are 14 total meridians. The remaining two meridians are called the "conception vessel" which deals with the front or anterior of the body, and the "governing vessel" which deals with the back or posterior of the body.

The meridians are evaluated in classical acupuncture for balanced Qi or life force/energy. Ideally the meridians have a good level of energy balanced between them. The practitioner seeks to find imbalances of the energy patterns of the meridian system, to which they attribute the cause of the condition. (Maciocia, 1989) When imbalances are found, the practitioner stimulates several acupuncture meridians with a needle or other means to restore balance to the system. (Mayor and Macozzi, 2011)

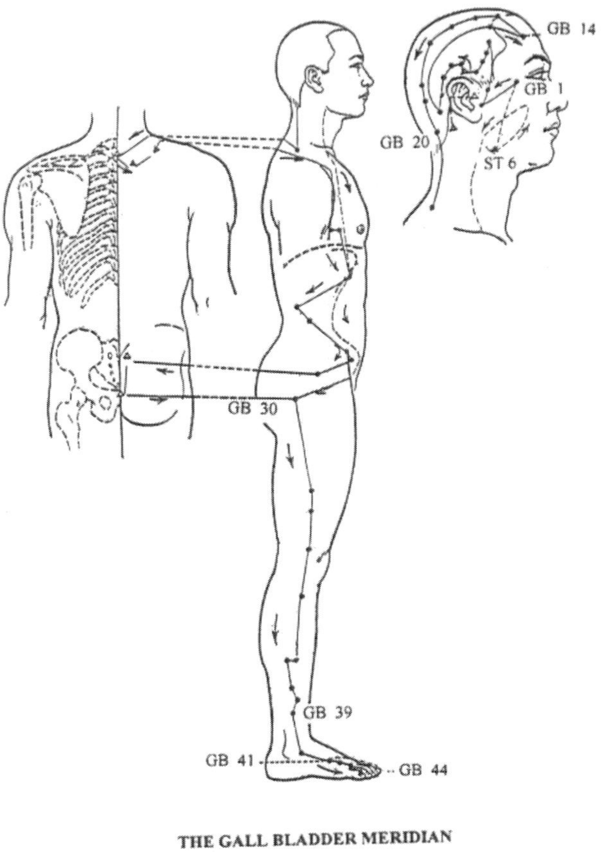

Figure 3. The Gall Bladder Meridian.

An imbalance of Qi within the meridian system can be responsible for a myriad of symptoms appearing in the body. Correcting this imbalance is the responsibility of the acupuncturist who may decide to use the standard application of needle or may use moxibustion (burning mugwort herb), laser, shiatsu, or a host of other different techniques used to balance the meridian system. It is for the above reasons we have decided to include Acupuncture and Oriental Medicine as one of the top Integrative practices to consider from when turning to an Integrative practice.

LONGEVITY

We would be remiss if we did not mention the fact that Oriental Medicine has always been based in wellness, prevention and longevity. Longevity in the West, relates to only to the duration of time (life), but not to the quality of life as is discussed in Eastern philosophy. Longevity, or "Chang Shou" in Chinese is used to imply not only length in years, but also the dedication of having quality of life unencumbered by pain and disease. In looking for ways to live long and vibrant lives, the ancient Chinese and Japanese found some interesting and effective endeavors. Self-care techniques were developed; like Qigong, Kung Fu, Tai Qi which used the ancient philosophy of acupuncture points for stimulation of Qi to enhance longevity in human life. Qigong, which is often spelled "Qi Gong" in the U.S., is a form of exercise for both body and spirit. It is practiced for exercise, relaxation, and promoting wellness. It involves slow flowing movements, a calm meditative state of mind, and deep rhythmic breathing. It is also a form or martial arts training. Kung Fu is a term familiar to most Americas as a martial art associated with fast movements, however the exercises practiced are for promoting the balance of Qi and wellness. Tai Qi is another martial art practiced both for defense and wellness. Some of the forms of Tai Qi involve slow fluid movements where breathing and meditation are important.

According to legend, Li Qing Yun was an Oriental Medicine Physician, herbal master and Qigong practitioner who lived to be 256 years old (1677-1933) and out lived nine of his emperors. His 1933 Obituary in *Time Magazine*, revealed his secrets to longevity: "Keep a quiet heart, sit like a tortoise, walk sprightly like a pigeon and sleep like a dog." Li lead a quiet life that consisted of never drinking hard liquor or smoking tobacco; he ate his plant-based meals at regular times and drank wolfberry (goji) tea. He slept early and awoke early and was said to have meditated for a few hours each day after his Qigong or Kung Fu exercises.

A study published in September 2013, in *The Lancet Oncology*, found that life style changes including adopting a plant-based diet, moderate exercise (walking for 30 minutes or more each day) and stress reduction (meditation or yoga) were associate with a significant increase in the telomere length (the part of the chromosome that affects cell aging). The study's lead author Dean Ornish, PhD has been on the cutting edge of nutrition science for many years. Telomeres are found at the end of our chromosomes and are believed to provide protection to the stranded molecules of DNA (like the binding around the tip of shoelaces to keep them from unraveling). Telomeres protect the ends of our chromosomes to help them remain stable.

Dr. Ornish's study showed that through a plant-based diet, 30 minutes of exercise each day, stress reduction techniques; yoga, Zen, prayer, etc. would significantly increase telomere length over the course of five years. Remarkably, that is the same lifestyle that Li Qing Yun advocated as a Chinese Medicine master hundreds of years ago.

A Bit of Philosophy with the Science

According to Tradition Chinese Medicine (TCM), we are all born with a finite amount of Qi and Jing (special Qi) that provides us with life force until our demise. As Dr. Deborah Waddell puts it in her article, *Longevity Utilizing Acupuncture, Chinese Medicine with Dietary and Life Style Changes*, think of Qi and Jing as your body's battery (positive and negative poles). This is your internal system of mind and body unified, each balancing the other in a healthy wellness state.

Chapter VI

EXAMPLES OF ACUPUNCTURE USE IN INTEGRATIVE MEDICINE

Dr. David Sniezek,
DC, MD, LAcup, FAAIM, FAAMA

USE IN ONCOLOGY

The principles of Integrative Medicine can be successfully applied to helping people affected by cancer. The use of IM among cancer patients ranges between 48% and 83%.[1, 2, 3] Therapies may enhance general immune function, aid in reducing symptoms such as pain, nausea, and anxiety, and help with detoxification. The IM practitioner recognizes that the biology of each person is unique and cancer will respond differently to therapies. For instance, certain supplements are clearly contraindicated in some cancer patients; however, some are acceptable at certain times and not at others. The route and time of delivery are also very important, as well as the coordination with standard therapy. Integrative cancer protocols are being developed to construct a logical and methodical plan for assessing treatment options, encourage

---

[1] DiGianni LM, Garber JE, Winer EP Complementary and alternative medicine use among women with breast cancer. *J Clin Oncol. 2002 Sep 15; 20(18 Suppl):34S-8S.*

[2] Richardson MA. Complementary and alternative therapy use in gynecologic oncology: implications for clinical practice. *Gynecol Oncol.* 2002 Mar; 84(3):360-2.

[3] Lu W, Dean-Clower E, Doherty-Gilman A, Rosenthal DS. The Value of Acupuncture in Cancer Care. Hematol Oncol Clin North Am. Aug 2008; 22(4): 631–viii.
(Retrieved November 29, 2014). http://www.ncbi.nlm.nih.gov/pmc/articles/PMC2642987/

identifying a patient advocate to help evaluate treatment choices, encourage standard oncology assessment and treatment recommendations, and engage in sequential exploration of biological markers. IM practitioners work to complement and enhance mainstream therapies. In conventional cancer treatment, the severe toxicity of the therapy kills the cancer cells directly. Unfortunately, especially in elderly people, the sum toxicity to all body tissues can be devastating, as widely discussed in the medical literature and media. Rebuilding the patient's biochemical performance brings about better health and sometimes-synergistic effects with the standard treatments that can become less toxic and more effective.

While there are many modalities being used by the IM practitioner for cancer patients, the most studied is acupuncture. The use of acupuncture by cancer patients is estimated to range between 1.7% and 31%.[4, 5] Many major cancer treatment centers have now incorporated Integrative Medicine, particularly medical acupuncture, into their programs. An increasing number of cancer centers in the U.S., including Dana-Farber Cancer Institute (DFCI) in Boston, Memorial Sloan-Kettering Cancer Center in New York, and M.D. Anderson Cancer Center in Houston are integrating acupuncture into cancer care. In November 2000, the Leonard P. Zakim Center for Integrative Therapies (Zakim Center) was established at Dana-Farber Cancer Institute (DFCI), a teaching hospital of Harvard Medical School, to provide both traditional and complementary therapies to patients of DFCI. The Zakim Center is named in memory of Lenny Zakim, a cancer patient and advocate for an integrative approach to cancer treatment. The mission of the Center is to educate and empower patients and staff by integrating the practice of complementary therapies into traditional cancer treatments.

In like manner, at Children's National Medical Center (CNMC) in Washington, DC, palliative care services are provided through the Pediatric Advanced Needs Assessment and Care (PANDA) Team, which is part of the Center for Cancer and Blood Disorders program. The multidisciplinary team of medical professionals assists health care team members, families, children, and adolescents with advanced illnesses. The team's goal is to prevent, reduce

---

[4] Morris KT, Johnson N, Homer L, Walts D. A comparison of complementary therapy use between breast cancer patients and patients with other primary tumor sites. *Am J Surg.* 2000 May; 179(5):407-11.

[5] Cui Y, Shu XO, Gao Y, Wen W, Ruan ZX, Jin F, Zheng W. Use of complementary and alternative medicine by Chinese women with breast cancer. *Breast Cancer Res Treat.* 2004 Jun; 85(3):263-70.

or soothe the symptoms of cancer and treatment experienced by patients in the advanced stages of illness.[6]

Medical acupuncture has been shown to be an effective and safe complementary method in palliative care (relieving pain or diminishing symptoms) for adults; however, very little has been studied or written regarding treatment of pain and other forms of suffering associated with life-threatening disorders for children and adolescents.[7, 8] Demand-induced establishment of medical acupuncture treatment specifically for children and adolescents was initiated at CNMC in 2008.

The initial impetus for incorporating medical acupuncture at CNMC included demand from patients' parents/guardians for more effective management of symptoms, including nausea, vomiting, and pain management. Given success of recent studies involving acupuncture for treating oncology-related symptoms, parents/guardians began requesting incorporation of related acupuncture treatments. This coupled with administrative initiatives to participate in a National Institutes of Health (NIH) study on medical acupuncture treatments for oncology set the stage for adopting and incorporating medical acupuncture treatments for palliative care primarily for oncology patients.

Prior to this project, there was no precedence for offering acupuncture or integrative medical treatments at CNMC. As such, CNMC retained an IM physician to design, develop and implement the components of an integrative medical unit, with primary interest in medical acupuncture, within the context of CNMC.

One of the most studied and practiced IM therapies is acupuncture. The NIH has defined acupuncture as

> ... a family of procedures involving stimulation of anatomical locations on the skin by a variety of techniques. The most studied mechanism of

---

[6] Children's National Medical Center, PANDA web page brochure. http://www.childrensnational.org/DepartmentsandPrograms/default.aspx?Type=Program&id=6140&SubType=ResourceForFamily&SubId=125&Name=Pediatric&Subname=PANDA%20Care%20Team%20Brochure , retrieved January 7, 2012.

[7] Johnstone P, Radiation Oncology Service, Naval Medical Center, San Diego, California 92134-1014 and Radiation Oncology Division, University of California, San Diego, California 92103; Gregory R Poston, Department of Anesthesiology; Richard C Niemtzow, Radiation Oncology Service and Department of Anesthesiology and Peter J Martin Head and Neck Surgery Service, Naval Medical Center, San Diego, California 92134-1014. *Palliative Medicine*, pg 16. 2002.

[8] Cohen L, M. Markman (eds.). *Integrative Oncology: Incorporating Complementary Medicine into Conventional Cancer Care*, Humana Press, Totowa, NJ., 2008.

stimulation of acupuncture points uses penetration of the skin by thin, solid, metallic needles, which are manipulated manually or by electrical stimulation.[9]

In the field of oncology, randomized clinical trials (RCT) have demonstrated that acupuncture is effective for chemotherapy-induced nausea and vomiting.[10] Research studies also suggest acupuncture may be helpful in managing cancer-related pain,[11] chemotherapy-related neutropenia[12] (which increases susceptibility to infection), cancer fatigue,[13] and radiation-induced xerostomia[14, 15] (dry mouth). Depression and anxiety have also been recently studied in an RCT with massage in combination with acupuncture in post-operative cancer patients.[16] This study revealed improved depressive mood in these patients as well as a short-lived improvement in tension and anxiety.

In the pediatric population, Integrative Medicine interventions such as acupuncture, chiropractic, massage, homeopathy, and dietary modifications are reportedly used by 25% to 20-30% of patients.[17, 18] Children with cancer, rheumatoid arthritis and cystic fibrosis report use of Integrative Medicine at

---

[9] NIH Consensus Conference. Acupuncture; *JAMA;* 1998. Nov 4, p. 1518.

[10] Dundee JW, Ghaly RG, Fitzpatrick KT, Abram WP, Lynch GA. Acupuncture prophylaxis of cancer chemotherapy-induced sickness. *J R Soc Med.* 1989 May; 82(5):268-71.

[11] Alimi D, Rubino C, Pichard-Léandri E, Fermand-Brulé S, Dubreuil-Lemaire ML, Hill C. Analgesic effect of auricular acupuncture for cancer pain: a randomized, blinded, controlled trial. *J Clin Oncol.* 2003 Nov 15; 21(22):4120-6.

[12] Lu W, Hu D, Dean-Clower E, Doherty-Gilman A, Legedza AT, Lee H, Matulonis U, Rosenthal DS. Acupuncture for chemotherapy-induced leukopenia: exploratory meta-analysis of randomized controlled trials. *J Soc Integr Oncol.* 2007 Winter; 5(1):1-10.

[13] Vickers AJ, Straus DJ, Fearon B, Cassileth BR. Acupuncture for postchemotherapy fatigue: a phase II study. *J Clin Oncol.* 2004 May 1; 22(9):1731-5.

[14] Blom M, Dawidson I, Fernberg JO, Johnson G, Angmar-Månsson B. Acupuncture treatment of patients with radiation-induced xerostomia. *Eur J Cancer B Oral Oncol.* 1996 May; 32B(3):182-90.

[15] Wong RK, Jones GW, Sagar SM, Babjak AF, Whelan T. A Phase I-II study in the use of acupuncture-like transcutaneous nerve stimulation in the treatment of radiation-induced xerostomia in head-and-neck cancer patients treated with radical radiotherapy. *Int J Radiat Oncol Biol Phys.* 2003 Oct 1; 57(2):472-80.

[16] Mehling WE, Jacobs B, Acree M, Wilson L, Bostrom A, West J, Acquah J, Burns B, Chapman J, Hecht FM. Symptom management with massage and acupuncture in postoperative cancer patients: a randomized controlled trial. *J Pain Symptom Manage.* 2007 Mar; 33(3):258-66.

[17] Davis MP, Darden PM. Use of conplementary and alternative medicine by children in the United States. *Arch of Pediatr Adolesc Med* 2003;157:393-6.

[18] Ottolini MC, Hamburger EK, Loprieato O, Coleman RH, Sachs HC, Madden R. et al. Complementary and alternative medicine use among children in the Washington, DC area. *Ambul Pediatr* 2001;1:122-5.

30-70%.[19, 20] According to the American Hospital Association, more than 37% of responding hospitals indicated they offer one or more CAM therapies, up from 26.5% of responding hospitals in 2005.[21] According to the same survey, 84% of hospitals indicated patient demand as the primary rationale in offering CAM services and 67% of survey respondents stated clinical effectiveness as their top reason. Medical acupuncture has been one of the most studied and is becoming increasingly popular in U.S. hospitals.

Despite increased popularity, a standard approach for addressing many of the obstacles in incorporating IM treatments in hospitals has yet to be established. Furthermore, practice guidelines for treatments such as medical acupuncture are still being developed.[22] A NCCAM study performed by the RAND Corporation highlighted a number of typical barriers in the design and setup of integrative medical treatments within the context of a hospital or health system. Some of these obstacles include accurate financial modeling, legal housing of integrative medical units and administrative capabilities.[23]

In the first 24 months of acupuncture integration, between November 2008 and November 2010, 28 patients with varying symptoms received medical acupuncture at the CNMC as inpatients and in the outpatient Hematology/Oncology Clinic. Conventional medical treatments were continued during acupuncture treatment.

Of the 14 patients referred for palliation of pain, 4 (28.5%) had no response. However, those with a response noted a mean value of 50% improvement. When that figure is averaged over all pain patients (including those who had no response), the mean improvement was 27%. Ten pain patients (60%) showed at least 30% improvement, and 4 patients (40%) showed at least 80% improvement. Duration of response was variable, but often resulted in reduced use of oral or intravenous painkiller. Furthermore, patients stated that they had improvement in their ability to perform daily activities and tolerate the side effects from the treatment of their illness. There were no adverse reactions to the acupuncture treatment.

---

[19] Grootenhuis MA, Last BF, de Graaf-Nijkerk JH, van der Wel M. Use of alternative treatment in pediatric oncology. *Cancer Nurs* 1998;21:282-8.

[20] Stern RC, Canda ER, Doershuk CF. Use of nonmedical treatment by cystic fibrosis patients. *J Adolesc Health* 1992;13:612-5.

[21] American Hospital Association website. Press Release. Latest Survey Shows More Hospitals Offering Complementary and Alternative Medicine Services. http://www.aha.org/presscenter/pressrel/2008/080915-pr-cam.shtml , retrieved February 4, 2012.

[22] Sniezek DP. Developing Practice Guidelines for Medical Acupuncture, *Medical Acupuncture,* Mary Ann Liebert, Inc., Volume 20, Number 3, p 137. 2008.

[23] Coulter ID. Hospital-Based Integrative Medicine: A Case Study of the Barriers and Factors Facilitating the Creation of a Center. *RAND Corporation*, Santa Monica, CA. 2008.

Of the 13 patients referred for chemotherapy-induced nausea and vomiting, 4 (30.8%) had no durable response. Responders experienced a mean 50% improvement, with 5 patients (55.5%) showing at least 30% improvement and 4 patients (44.4%) with at least 80% improvement.

Table 2. Demographics of the population administered the questionnaire

Gender	14 male	
	14 female	
Age	mean	20
	range	18 mo - 27 yrs
Visits	mean	10
	range	1-30
141 Total visits		
	pain	52%
	nausea, vomiting	42%
	other (fatigue, insomnia, etc)	6%

All patients in the smaller groups referred for fatigue and insomnia experienced some relief of their symptoms. The mean improvement was 80% for fatigue and 85% for insomnia.

When surveyed about acupuncture, 21 responses were received from 24 patients (or family members). When asked the global question about the value of acupuncture, 21 patients (100%) considered it important or very important. Those percentages continued when patients were asked whether CNMC should continue acupuncture: 100% recommended continuing the service.

As shown by the results, there is significant consumer pull-through and on-going demand for medical acupuncture treatment in hospital-based palliative oncology care for children. Additionally, demand for medical acupuncture has spread to other hospital programs including orthopedic, neurology, and medicine departments.

In summary, Integrative Medicine is poised to enter into traditional US healthcare organizations, albeit, slowly. Recent evidence-based studies on safety, efficacy, and cost further confirm that IM approaches have been underutilized. With growing interest from the public sector, the scientific community and healthcare organizations, it is anticipated that there will be significant increase in interest for hospital administrators and medical staff leadership to incorporate IM in their facilities. While this transition is encouraging; it is also important to point out the need to develop or follow established procedures and protocols where they exist and seek advice from an IM healthcare consultant where a precedent has not been established.

USE IN SPORTS MEDICINE: OVERUSE INJURIES TO THE KNEE

The principles of Integrative Medicine can also be successfully applied to helping elite professional athletes. Integrative Medicine practitioners have been treating professional athletes for many years in their private practices; however, they have not transitioned into the training rooms or on the sidelines of professional sports, particularly basketball, until recently. Professional athletes are highly motivated to find ways to optimize muscle recovery and performance without the use of drugs. Acupuncture has been effective in this area and is best applied immediately before and after workouts and games. The result has been that, as in the case of other areas of medicine that were once only considered under the purview of allopathic (conventional) physicians, Integrative Medicine practitioners have now been invited by players and owners to interact with the professional athletes where they work, in the training rooms, on the field and on the courtsides. One of the major professional sports industries in the U.S. is professional basketball, and one of the most common conditions affecting elite basketball players is overuse injuries to the knee. We will discuss the use of acupuncture in the setting of a professional basketball team training room.

INTEGRATIVE MEDICINE AND THE WASHINGTON WIZARDS

The initial impetus for incorporating Integrative Medicine and medical acupuncture in the Washington Wizard's training room arose from the head trainer's interest in helping individual players manage their symptoms, including pain, swelling, stiffness, and improved recovery and performance more effectively without the use of drugs. During the regular season players have a very busy schedule and have difficulty making regular doctor appointments. As a matter of convenience for the players, acupuncture and other IM services were coordinated with the other medical staff and administered in the training room at practices, games or on the road.

During the 2012-2014 NBA seasons, Integrative Medicine services, with particular interest in chiropractic and medical acupuncture, were sought for injuries sustained during practices or games. One of the most prevalent injuries encountered were overuse injuries to the knee.

Overuse injuries to the knee in professional basketball is a debilitating condition for which no standard treatment strategy has yet been established. While the pathophysiology of overuse injuries is well understood, the nature of the pain mechanisms remains unclear leaving treatment choices challenging.

Few studies have been published on the epidemiology of overuse injuries to the professional basketball player.[24, 25, 26, 27, 28] Several recent studies have been published regarding injury rates in high school and college basketball.[29, 30, 31] Compared to high school and college, the NBA players compete on a longer court, for a greater number of minutes per game and times per week, for a longer season, and at an older age.

In a study of injuries afflicting NBA players over a 17-year period, lower extremity injuries make up 62.4% of all injuries and account for 72.3% of games missed.[56] According to Dracos, et al., the most games missed were related to patellofemoral inflammation (n, 10,370: 17.5%).[32]

Management of overuse injury to the knee is currently unclear, and, as such, alternative methods are continually being explored. Acupuncture in

---

[24] Drakos, MC, Domb, B, Allen AA. Injury in the National Basketball Association, Sports Health. Table 2. 2010 July; 2(4) 284-290.

[25] Zelisko JA, Noble HB, Porter M. A comparison of men's and women's professional basketball injuries. Am J Sports Med. 1982;10:297-299.

[26] Starkey C. Injuries and illnesses in the national basketball association: a 10-year perspective. J Athl Train. 2000;35:161-167.

[27] Lombardo S, Sethi PM, Starkey C. Intercondylar notch stenosis is not a risk factor for anterior cruciate ligament tears in professional male basketball players: an 11-year prospective study. Am J Sports Med. 2005;33:29-34.

[28] Henry JH, Lareau B, Neigut D. The injury rate in professional basketball. Am J Sports Med. 1982;10:16-18.

[29] Messina DF, Farney WC, DeLee JC. The incidence of injury in Texas high school basketball: a prospective study among male and female athletes. Am J Sports Med. 1999;27:294-299.

[30] Emery CA, Meeuwisse WH, McAllister JR. Survey of sport participation and sport injury in Calgary and area high schools. Clin J Sport Med. 2006;16:20-26.

[31] Meeuwisse WH, Sellmer R, Hagel BE. Rates and risks of injury during intercollegiate basketball. Am J Sports Med. 2003;31:379-385.

[32] Drakos, MC, Domb, B, Allen AA. Injury in the National Basketball Association, Sports Health. Table 2. 2010 July; 2(4) 286.

medicine has grown into a large, popular, and visible part of medical practice during the past decade. Western medical scholars have advanced the science of acupuncture to the extent that it is now being utilized for the treatment of not only neurologic and musculoskeletal conditions but also psychological problems.

Sports medicine is used by a variety of health care professionals and is practiced in a number of venues with overlapping but distinct areas of expertise. These may include physicians, athletic trainers, acupuncturists, massage therapists, podiatrists, dietitians, psychologists, exercise physiologists, chiropractors, surgeons, physical therapists and several other specialties. Each health care discipline practicing under the umbrella of sports medicine has the same goal of rehabilitating the injured athlete back to full participation and function.

Integrative Medicine has also grown into a very large, popular and highly visible area of medicine during the past decade and has become established in rehabilitation medicine and is now beginning to enter into sports medicine at all levels. Below is an overview of sports Integrative Medicine principles and practice for medical acupuncturists who are evaluating and treating elite professional basketball players with knee injuries.

Sports medicine acupuncture contains both Traditional Chinese Medicine (TCM) and sports medicine diagnostic techniques to view the patient's injury from each of these different perspectives. The goal is to accurately assess the mechanism and severity of the patient's musculoskeletal complaint. This is accomplished by using a combination of orthopedic special tests, range of motion, manual muscle testing and palpation to identify the injured tissue. These techniques used to assess local stagnation are joined with TCM differential diagnosis, providing a paradigm of the athlete's local injury and overall health (Qi, Blood, Yin, Yang, Shen). Shen refers to spirit or mental energy. The objective of this combination, sports Integrative Medicine, is to address the athlete's healing potential thereby strengthening the patient, and as a result, decreasing injury rehabilitation time. Getting the athletes back to their desired activity, enhancing performance, and preventing re-injury through treatment and education are the goals.

The forces across the knee from the combination of running, jumping, cutting, pivoting and sudden acceleration and deceleration on a hard court are unique to basketball.[33] This situation predisposes basketball players to overuse

[33] Yost, JG, Ellfeldt HJ: Basketball Injuries. In *The Lower Extremity & Spine in Sports Medicine*. St. Louis, CV Mosby, 1986. pp 1140-1455.

injuries to the knee. In addition, these injuries are responsible for 66% of games missed. The vast majority of sports injuries are due to acute macrotrauma or chronic repetitive microtrauma. Each type of injury has its own unique features that require specific diagnostic and treatment approaches.

Diagnosis of overuse injuries to the knee is typically done by physical examination. The use of various imaging devices, including musculoskeletal diagnostic ultrasound, x-ray and MRI can provide additional information and guide treatment. Ultrasound imaging has become increasingly more popular among sports medicine specialists because of the higher quality image, portability, safety and the ability to obtain real-time evaluations in the training room. Below is an ultrasound evaluation of patellar tendon tendinosis.[34]

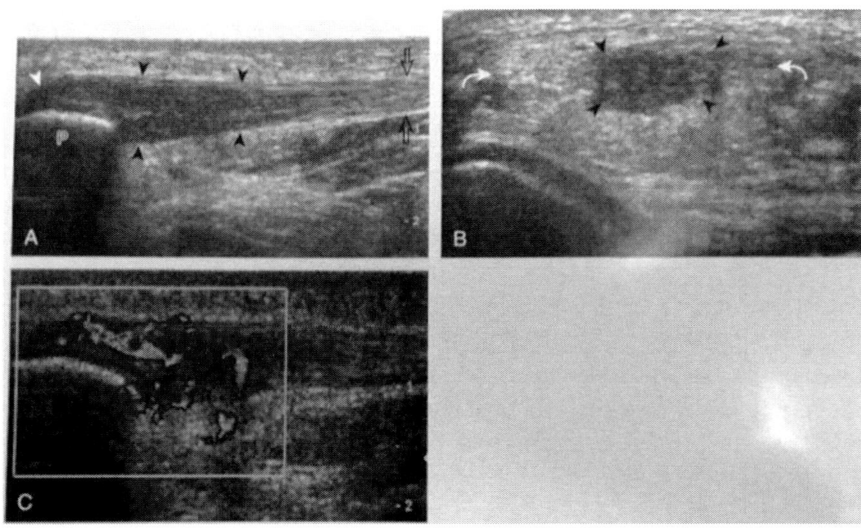

Ultrasound images (A) long axis and (B) short axis to proximal patellar tendon show hypoechoic tendon swelling with intact fibers (arrowheads). Note the normal distal patellar tendon thickness (open arrows) in A and width of the patellar tendon (curved arrows) in B. Corresponding long axis color Doppler images is shown in (C). P. patella.

[34] Jacobson Jon A. *Fundamentals of Musculoskeletal Ultrasound,* Edition 2. Philadelphia, PA, Elsevier Saunders, 2013, p 238.

During ultrasound, tendinosis appears as hypoechoic swelling with continuous tendon fibers.[35] Superimposed interstitial tears may be identified by the presence of hypochoic or anechoid clefts. Color Doppler imaging can identify hyperemia from neovascularity that is associated with pain.[36] Other tendon discontinuity can be confirmed by dynamic imaging, such as partial or full-thickness tears. Osgood-Schlatters disease, a painful condition that affects the distal patellar tendon insertion from repetitive trauma in an adolescent can also be identified using ultrasound. Ultrasound can be used to identify many overuse injuries to the knee and is a valuable diagnostic tool in the right hands.

PRINCIPLES OF INTEGRATIVE REHABILITATION

There are a variety of acupuncture techniques that can be applied successfully in sports medicine. Selection of which system to apply is dependent upon many factors that can include the oriental and medical diagnosis, acuteness of the condition, location of the complaint, and when treatment is being administered (e.g., immediately before a game, at half-time, after a game, off-season, etc.) Needless to say, a practical understanding of the above techniques is useful in helping to alleviate pain and stiffness. Rather than attempt to describe each technique, an example of a typical acupuncture treatment on a professional basketball player with an acute left knee overuse injury before a game is described below.

GAME-DAY: EXAMPLE OF PRE-GAME POINT SELECTION AND RATIONALE

In this example, a left-hand dominant shooting guard sustained a left patellar (knee) tendonitis that started in a game one week ago. The pain kept him from playing his normal minutes and had affected his overall performance. He would like to be able to better manage his pain without medication so that he can safely participate in the game that starts in one hour. Examination revealed pain to palpation over the patellar tendon with no

---

[35] Felus J, Kowalczyk B, Lejman T: Sonographic evaluation of the injuries after traumatic patellar dislocation in adolescents. *J Pediatr Orthop.* 28:397-402 2008 18520273

[36] Hoksrud A, Ohberg L, Alfredson H, et al.: Color Doppler ultrasound findings in patellar tendinopathy (jumper's knee). *Am J Sports Med.* 36:1813-1820 2008 18753682

swelling or instability. All imaging and testing by an orthopedist was normal and the player was cleared to participate in today's game. Pain was localized to the distal patellar insertion at the tibia.

Acupoint selection is important before games. In this scenario the acronym "fans" was recommended. As such, points selected were fewer, away from the site of pain, non-depleting, and of short duration. Because the pain was very localized in the left knee of a left-handed shooting guard, the acupuncture treatment technique chosen was a combination of Opposite-Side / Opposite Extremity. An ashi point near the right LI-11 (the acupuncture point in is the arm) was identified and quick pain relief was successful. Taking into consideration as many aspects of the athlete's condition is crucial in obtaining the best outcome and trust of the patient. The use of the acronym "fans" to proceed with treatment during a pre-game treatment has been successful. Below is a brief explanation of why this technique was selected.

Fewer points. Generally, speaking only a few points are required before a game. Athletes tend to be more yang and require fewer points to move energy. As such, the least number of inputs to achieve the desired effect is recommended. The number of needles typically will range from 1 to 6. Too many points could result in general energy depletion, which should usually be avoided before game time. In some instances, such as with anxiety or nervous energy, additional points may be attempted but only for a short duration, 5 to 10 minutes.

Away from the site of pain. It is best to use point(s) that are away from the site of pain.[37] Placing a foreign object, such as an acupuncture needle, or even acupressure, over an area of inflammation may cause a flare-up that is out of proportion to the stimulation. This type of flare-up should be avoided immediately prior to a game. Site selection for left patellar tendon symptoms is the right elbow, such as LI-11 or ashi point near the classical point. Typically only one needle at precisely the correct right elbow ashi point is necessary.

Non-depleting points. Stimulation of a sedating point or depletion of an activation point can result in fatigue. This response immediately prior to a game can negatively influence performance. Therefore, careful selection of acupoints and method of stimulation is important.

Short treatment duration. The typical treatment for pre-game or during the game is less than 10 minutes. Longer treatment times may deplete energy.

---

[37] Tan R, Rush, S. *Twelve and Twelve in Acupuncture.* Advanced Principles and Techniques. Unique Point Applications and Case Studies for Effective Pain Relief, 2nd Edition. San Diego, CA. August 1996, p 106.

Shorter treatment times are often sufficient to reduce pain. With experience, significant pain reduction can be achieved in a matter of seconds.

This is only one example of how acupuncture can be used in sports medicine to improve safe and effective performance without the use of medication. As mentioned previously, acupuncture has additional benefits after games and practices that will help the athlete with muscle recovery as well. Needless to say there are many more ways in which acupuncture and other Integrative Medicine techniques can be of benefit for not only the elite professional basketball player but all athletes. Integrative Medicine is being used by professional football players, Olympians, swimmers, hockey players, and by professional and non-professional athletes in virtually every sport.

The application of Integrative Medicine in sports will continue to increase for many of the same reasons as in other areas of medicine, including pediatric oncology. Incentives to ease pain and other untoward symptoms, improve function, quality of life, and performance by natural means are universal goals of Integrative Medicine.

Integrative Medicine continues to be a growing and important part of mainstream medicine in the U.S. Many factors contributed to this phenomenon, including the U.S. healthcare crisis, sluggish economy, and divided politics. Moreover, the founding principles of Integrative Medicine that include demand-driven treatments and patient-centered practices have facilitated the incorporation of Integrative Medicine into traditional medicine in unexpected areas. As shown in pediatric oncology in a major teaching hospital and sports medicine with an NBA team, Integrative Medicine has made significant progress and contributions. It is clear that Integrative Medicine has improved treatment efficacy, efficiency, and response to consumer demand while being fiscally sustainable which, in turn, has improved our healthcare system.

Chapter VII

NUTRITION

John L. Stump, DC, PhD, EdD
and Donna Retzlaff-Roberts, PhD

"Except our own thoughts, there is nothing absolutely in our power."

REN'E DESCARTES (1596- 1650)

A PERSONAL CHOICE

Another important practice that goes with our Integrative approach to wellness is Applied Nutrition. The principles that underlie what we are going to discuss are the same basic proteins, fats and carbohydrates that we learn in our high school and undergraduate education in health and nutrition class. The only difference is in the application and understanding of the use of the proteins, fats and carbohydrates or should we say the misuse! We will discuss the personal choices of the vitamins, minerals, enzymes and amino acids in ways you may not recognize because most people don't think of these facts when they eat their food.

When asked, most people think of the current health care crisis in the Unites States as a health insurance disaster. Although the deficiency of health care insurance is a problem for many, it pales in comparison to the real calamity… in American's general health status. This crisis affects all segments of the population, young and old, rich and poor, over weight and underweight.

To Where Did America's Health Disappear?

- Governmental Agencies: The FDA, USDA, etc.,
- Health Care Industry: Current medical control of health care practices
- Pharmaceutical Industry: The manipulation of drug prices
- Food Industry: Unhealthy food choices in the market place
- Farm Industry: The high percentage of unhealthy and toxic sprays used.

Each of these points is part of perpetuating the issue, but none are the primary cause. The tangible reason behind the health care crisis is an individual's poor choices and routine, mostly in the areas of food, exercise and lifestyle management.

This advances to health related issues such as:

- Overweight
- Obesity
- Depression
- Hypertension
- Fatigue
- Arthritis
- Inflammation
- Sleep apnea
- Blood lipid abnormalities

- Stroke
- Heart disease
- Female and males hormone imbalances
- Metabolic syndrome
- Fatty liver
- Cancers
- Gall Bladder dysfunction
- Skin disease
- Acid reflux
- Type II diabetes
- Pain syndromes

Regardless of where we want to place the blame it really comes down to taking personal responsibility for our health. This means taking a personal obligation to educate and apply that knowledge to the choices we make for ourselves and our family and friends when necessary.

Obesity…literally one of our biggest health issues!

Today, one of the issues looming over or should we say in front of the American people and others around the globe is obesity. In fact, it is at epidemic proportions:

- 66% of adults are overweight
- 34% of adults are obese
- 16% of youth are obese or overweight
- These stats are even worse when we look at our Southern states!

Millions and maybe billions are spent to find the answer to the obesity epidemic and this is just the tip of the iceberg from a health science perspective. Obesity leads to diabetes, diabetes leads to possible circulatory, heart or stroke issues and we all know where the death statistics are there!

To emphasize this even more, let me give you a few health statistics over the past century.

- *Sugar* consumption has increased from 5 pounds per person per year to 158 pounds.

- *Processed* grain consumption, such as chips, crackers, pretzels, etc., has increased by 62 pounds per person yearly.
- *Red* meat consumption increased by 60 pounds annually.
- *Cheese and dairy* consumption increased by 28 pounds per year.
- *Soft drink* consumption increased by 53 gallons per year.
- *500 calories* per day has been added to our diets.
- *TV and Video watching* has increased to 4 hours per day.

It doesn't take a genius to figure out how the overweight and obesity problem came about. Simply put, the lack of lifestyle, exercise and poor eating habits are the problem. If we would all return to a more natural diet like what our grandparents ate, rich in fresh vegetables and fruit while avoiding the processed foods in can, bottle and box. Plus, staying active which means a half hour of walking, running or your choice of activity each day in the sunshine when possible. Yes, there are other factors involved, but to accomplish this simple task, has taken the American public more than 20 years since it was presented by the experts in the American Public Health Forum.

YOUR GRANDMOTHER WARNED YOU

During our youth and our grandparent's childhood, American diets were quite different. If one could take a peek in a grocery store back in history you would find fresh, local fruit and vegetables, seeds, nuts, grains and honey. Some fresh local dairy, like eggs, butter and cheese was available. Most of the time a local grocery store would have a butcher shop or meat market. As a matter-of-fact you may have worked in such a grocery store. Let's call it Thompson's Market which serves the community of Henderson in a county on the Eastern Shore of Maryland. Your small community of Henderson may be typical of many small communities. In this grocery store you could get fresh vegetables, fruit, eggs and different meats that you may cut yourselve. Everyone came to the little grocery store each week to stock up on the staples. This is not the case today, just ride through your old stompin' grounds and you will see the little mom and pop grocery stores in each of the little towns have closed. Now everyone goes to the larger cities in the surrounding areas to shop for the family groceries.

TODAY'S FOOD PRESENTATION

In the typical store today all the products are shipped in from all over the U.S., Canada, Mexico and other countries. There are few, if any, fresh local products except in a few special market stores; like *Whole Foods* and *Fresh Market*. The things you find now were not even considered for store shelves a few decades ago.

A Grandmother and neighbor, a Cherokee medicine woman who lived to be 96, warned that our food was getting too far away from nature and people would begin paying the price with health problems. Her life was a story of natural health according to Indian legend. Her herbal and folk remedies were from the Appalachians. Again there isn't sufficient time or space to devote to her remedies and philosophy but suffice it to say she helped many get on the path to natural health and wellness care many years ago.

Today, you find much that is added to our foods that's questionable or actually known to be harmful but somehow it's in the foods and drinks. The following list is just a few of the things we can think of off the cuff:

- Hormones in injected meats
- Processed foods
- Fast foods
- Junk foods
- Imported foods of questionable origin (for example farm raised fish from China)

With these altered food choices a completely different diet is now used in America. It is termed the SAD diet (Standard American Diet). The foods found in the SAD are found to have many inadequacies and imbalances.

- An excessive amount of questionable food items such as salt, sugar, and filler.
- Small amounts of real vegetables, fruit or enzymes.
- Lack of nutrient rich foods due to over cooking and processing.
- Copious amounts of additives and preservatives for shelf life.

Meat What's the Real Story?

Most people don't even understand the amount of meat protein they should have each day. It is really only 4-6 ounces per day depending on the person's size, energy expenditure, metabolism, etc. but the average American consumes more than twelve ounces per day! That's more than double the recommended amount. A lot of people are not aware that too much protein can have its detriment as well.

- Excess protein makes the pancreas decrease enzymes. Enzymes are necessary for the digestion of food and absorption of vitamins and minerals.
- Excess protein requires an extreme amount of vitamin and minerals to be used in digestion leading to a possible B6, zinc, calcium, or magnesium deficiency.
- Uric acid builds up in the body and causes gout and contributes to arthritis.
- Excessive protein causes the stomach to produce less acid causing digestion to slow, triggering possible acid reflux and other digestive problems.

There are other debated issues with red meat consumption but none with an absolute link like heart disease, stroke, obesity, diabetes and cancer. I think the most important consideration is the quality of the cut of meat that one decides to consume. Of course, we have all heard of too much of a good thing!

Man Made Food

The wisdom of man so far has not been in replicating food. All the processed, refined, preserved and denatured foods produced by man are inferior to mother nature's. Our American diet is more deficient now than ever before.

Ancient Theory on Food

We all know, for food to be consumed it must be placed in the mouth and chewed or masticated. This act alone tells us the basic diet to use when the selection of food is considered. Before we go into the selection of the human diet let's look at some of our animal friends.

Dog is man's best friend or so the story goes. What the dog selects naturally and genetically determines its health and longevity. But how does the food become selected when the animal is domesticated? The knowledge has been handed down for generations that your dog is a carnivore and this is determined by what… the animal's teeth and its diet. Yes, when you look into the mouth of your dog you will see that it is filled with incisors, premolars, and molars and yes canines. Even though the teeth may sound like your human teeth when they are examined they are shaped and function as supportive teeth of the dominant canines. They are carnivorous but today with all the pet foods being shifted to plant based it's hard to say what's going to happen in the canine world.

On the other hand, if we look into the mouth of a herbivore like a horse you will see that it is filled with another type of tooth called premolar and molars and has few canine teeth. Why is this? Well, you have carnivores (meat eaters) and herbivores (plant eaters) and a few like the human that consume both, the omnivores.

When one is taught biology in high school one of the assignments always given is to name as many animals in the world that were meat eaters or plant eaters, and to do this with no outside help. Then discuss what, how and why of the animal world are of each type. When the assignment was complete the students realized that genetics make the whole world different through environment and behavior.

Getting back to the human, when we look in the mouth we find the same teeth in most adults, incisors (8), canine (4) and molars (20) for a total of 32 teeth. If we further break this down it comes out to be:

Canine =12.5% or 1/8 of 32 are our meat and dairy teeth (tearing).

Incisors = 25% or ¼ of 32 are our vegetable and fruit teeth.

Molars =62.5% or 5/8 of 32 are our grain, seed and nut teeth.

Only 12.5 percent are canine tearing teeth so the ancient Oriental philosophers felt that was to be our meat and dairy allotment. Then there is 25 percent biting teeth called the incisors and are considered to be the vegetable and fruit teeth. The clear majority happens to be the molars at 62.5 percent said to be the grinding teeth of grains, seeds and nuts.

This is an ancient theory introduced to the West by George Ohsawa and Michio Kushi of Macrobiotic prominence. It involves how humans developed diets and eating habits and is pretty close to the proper balance according to scientific investigation done nearly a century ago by western food scientists. Remember, ancient man did not consume any of the processed, man-made foods we consume today, only whole all natural, organic foods.

Even 50 years ago Macrobiotic followers understood the problems of stripping off the outside layer of rice (whole brown rice) and developing new white rice would bring to the world's population. Brown (whole) rice was the staple for over a billion people. However, a few years after the introduction of white rice on the population of the world, there was an increase in nutritional based disease and that number has continued to grow each year due to the over indulgence of humans for fast, over processed, chemical filled food.

I wished we had time to discuss this at greater length but for those of you that are interested go to www.macrobiotics.com and read about the history and development of this organization.

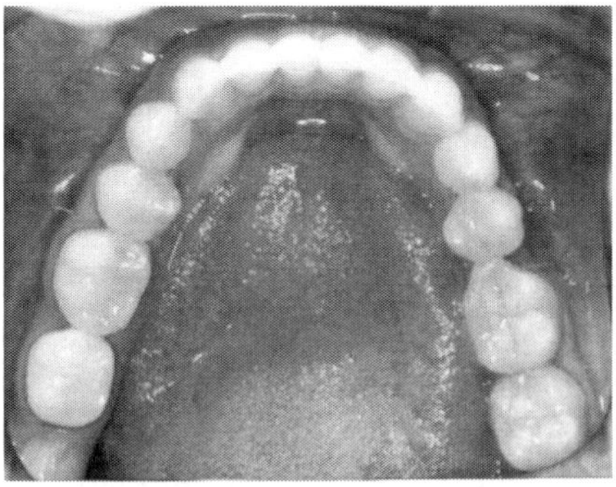

Figure 4. Can you name the teeth and note the structure of the adult tooth?

This is another reason when an individual goes to an acupuncturist or Chinese Medicine practitioner or an Integrative practitioner, the examination begins with observation. Just the appearance tells the practitioner a great deal about the health of the individual. The smile, teeth and the mouth are the beginning picture of the health and wellness of the individual. We will delve into this a little more as we venture further into the practice of integrative wellness and whole health.

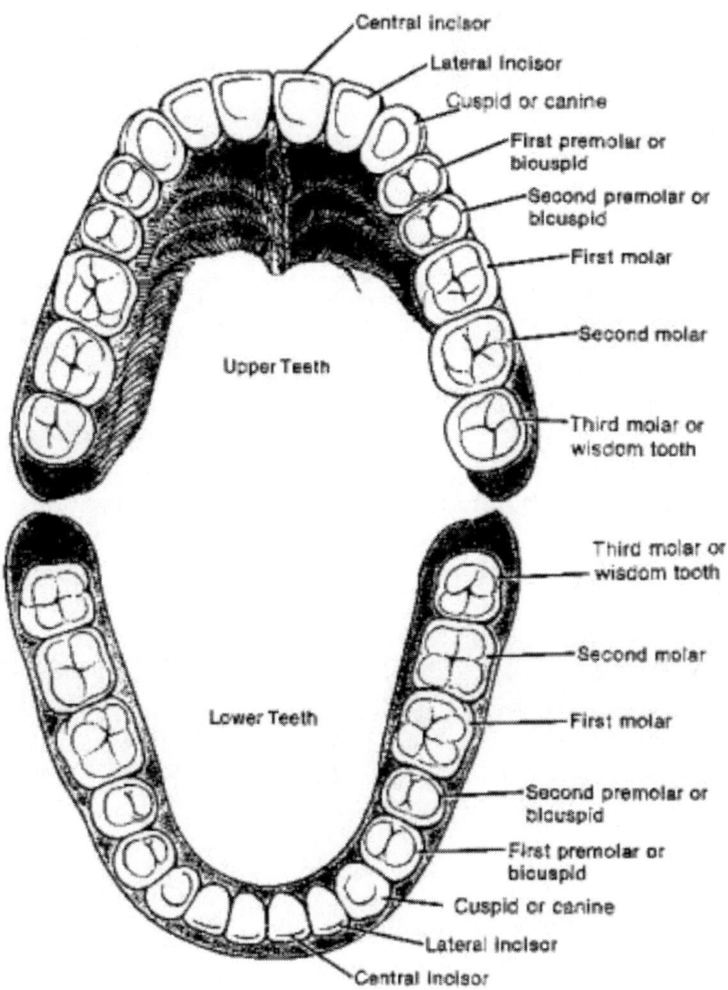

Figure 5. The Adult Human Teeth Arrangement.

Man's Attempt to Improve Food

For decades, man has tried to improve upon natural, real, whole foods, only to find there is no way to advance the perfection of nature. For instance, prior to World War II, food factories in Demark were "processing" brown rice and wheat flour to make white rice and white wheat flour. Once the war made it impossible to complete manufacturing of the products, they noticed they were selling more brown rice and wheat. A study done after the war indicated the death rate in Denmark went down 39%, as well as, a marked decline in cancer, diabetes and kidney disease.

Despite such history, illustrations and hundreds of studies, processed foods make up nearly 90 percent of the American diet. Most processed foods are laden with:

- Sweeteners
- Salts
- Artificial flavors
- Factory-created fats
- Added colorings
- Chemicals for altered texture
- Preservatives

Processed foods not only have additives, but frequently vital nutrients have been stripped away during the manufacturing process. These include enzymes, vitamins and minerals. This is where most of the trouble comes when the companies try to "guess" what should be put in or taken out of a food during this process.

Whole natural foods are complete and flawless foods. Eating a wide variety of vegetables, fruits and whole grains normally would give your body everything it needs for good health and wellness. However, the Standard American Diet that is attempting to sustain most Americans will not… and this is where health is beginning to be lost.

Adulterated Food

Adulterated food is food that is contaminated, polluted or mixed with an impure substance. Adulterated is another descriptive word that the Standard

American Diet (SAD) system has brought into our food vocabulary, even when we are eating fruits and vegetables that really don't have enough nutritive value to be called "food." Most are cooking the food to death...our death.

When plants are heated above approximately 107 degrees Fahrenheit, certain enzymes in food are destroyed. Vitamin C is adulterated if food is heated above 130 degrees F. But you are told that pasteurization at (145 degrees F) is considered good. However, it destroys many nutrients within the food. The solution is to eat raw fruits and vegetables whenever possible. That does not mean they can't be washed and slightly steamed for easier digestive processing for those that have digestive issues.

The Center for Disease Control (CDC) says to eat five serving of vegetables and fruit each day. More aggressive literature suggests nine serving each day. As a general rule eat three vegetables to each fruit. Today, at the low end of the scale, less than 33% of Americans are getting their daily allowance of whole fruit and vegetables.

The Standard American Diet (SAD)

The diet that has been pushed on the American public is sad indeed. It is high in calories and low in nutritive value and consists of foods such as:

- Refined flour
- Refined sugar
- Refined cooking oil
- Soft drinks
- Margarine
- Refined salts
- Additives & enhancers
- Preservatives
- Chemicals
- Undetermined substances

In order to be healthy, we need to replace low nutrient processed foods with high nutrient whole foods such as:

- Vegetables
- Fruits
- Non-processed meats
- Fish
- Wild game
- Whole grains
- Nuts and seeds
- Fresh spices
- Natural herbs

A healthy body needs a diet high in enzymes, antioxidants, vitamins and minerals this is the reason for the emphasis on whole foods.

- Vitamins and minerals are fuel for our body functions
- Enzymes must be present for healthy digestion, absorption and metabolism.
- Antioxidants regulate cells to keep them healthy and eliminate free radicals that may cause cell mutation.

When your body doesn't have the nutrients necessary, cell and tissue atrophy begin and this is the foundation of the aging process along with diseases and chronic conditions mentioned up to this point.

The Blood Sugar Issue

Another huge issue in nutrition in the 21st century is Blood Sugar. It seems like almost everyone who comes in the office can be placed in a category with a blood sugar issue. Many young people consume much too much sugar, but have never had their blood sugar tested. So when someone is over 30 and has their blood sugar tested for the first time, they are surprised to find their blood sugar is in a pre-diabetic or insulin resistant range. At this point something must be done to prevent the oncoming diabetes. In the worst case scenario, one finds oneself in the Type II diabetic range. Then you only have a choice of insulin dependency or try to manage the condition with diet and exercise. Usually, the patient is now under a physician's care that specializes in endocrine problems or the GP prescribes insulin because the patient can't or won't manage the disease through diet and exercise.

However, there is another solution to your '*sugar shock*'... proper nutrition. By following the correct recommendations from your Integrative practitioner a person can get themselves back on tract within six months of the diagnosis without the need for prescriptions and/or medications.

FEDERAL FOOD AND DRUG ADMINISTRATION (FDA)

James Gormley is a leader of the natural health movement in America today and an award-winning journalist. He is passionate advocate for natural and whole foods. For more than 20 years, he has been at the forefront in the fight against government restriction of dietary supplements and for the transparency in the food industry, and has twice participated in America's trade delegation to the United Nations Codex Alimentarius Commission, advocating for health freedom.

Gormley's editorial positions have included editor-in-chief of *Better Nutrition* and editorial director for the *Vitamin Retailer Magazine* Group. He now serves as both vice president and senior policy advisor for Citizens for Health and as a scientific advisory board member with the Natural Health Research Institute.

His latest book, *Health at Gunpoint: The FDA's Silent War Against Health Freedom,* poses a strong stance against government interference in our rights to information about and access to healthy food choices and whole food supplements.

This book should be on every health conscious persons reading list. We all must become educated health and wellness advocates.

Water

The old recommendations of eight glasses of water each day is good but doesn't go far enough. Assuming an 8 ounce glass, that would be 64 ounces or 2 quarts per day. The most accurate measurement of the hydration needed in term of pure water should be – to aim for one half of your body weight in ounces of water each day up to three quarts.

For example, an individual of 180 pounds should consume 90 ounces of water each day which is about 2.8 quarts per day. Of course, the number of ounces should be increased if you are in a particularly hot environment or if your body activity-level has you sweating more than normal, such as during summer camps of football, soccer, running a triathlon or marathon and any other such physical activity.

In addition you want to be should it's pure water, not tap water, mineral or vitamin water, some of these contain hormones, viruses, bacteria, chlorine, and a host of chemicals that you do not want in your body. A good practice is to put two or three slices of lemon in each glass of water consumed. This not only tastes good, it also increases the pH level in your body.

> Since the subject of pH has been brought up (pH- In chemistry, pH is a measure of the acidity or basicity of an aqueous solution.) Solutions with a pH less than **7** are said to be acidic and solutions with a pH greater than **7** are basic or alkaline. Pure water has a pH very close to **7**.

When salvia is measured in the human body with pH strips the average person now measures about 6.2 - 6.6, this is very acid. Our oral human salvia should measure 7.2-7.4, much more alkaline for a healthy individual that is into wellness. Since we are human, our enzymatic, immunologic, and repair mechanisms all function their best in this alkaline range. However, our metabolic processes---the processes of living, tissue repair, and the metabolism of food---produce a great deal of acid. In order to maintain our internal alkaline state, we need a few tools. These tools are all around us: oxygen, water, and acid-buffering minerals.

Examples:

Exercise - When we exercise or move around, we produce lactic acid and carbon dioxide. Lactic acid is by its very nature acid and carbon dioxide becomes acidic, turning into carbonic acid and water.

Digestion - Digestion of foods generates acids. For example, phosphoric acid and sulfuric acid are produced from the metabolism of the phosphorus and sulfur contained in many foods, such as, meats, grains, and beans.

Immune Responses - Immune system responses, such as allergies and hypersensitivities, directly and indirectly generate substantial amounts of acidic products in our bodies.

Many lifestyle and environment factors also influence acid-alkaline balance. Remember pure water is needed in each of these instances to help with the chemical and mechanical breakdown in the body to flush out these excess acids.

Be an Educated Consumer

If you watch TV or are on the Internet, read, or listen to the radio you known that you are bombarded with advertisements 24-7. The food industry uses these methods to get you to buy the adulterated foods we discussed earlier. In other words, the food industry has gotten you to eat unhealthy foods and believe you are doing the right thing for your body!

You may not believe this at first but stick with us here. When was the last time you saw a junk food advertisement on TV? What about vegetables and fruit? Junk food is consistently advertised and simple fruits and vegetables are rarely advertised. We know that whole foods, fruit and vegetables are good for us but we continue to buy the foods that are advertised.

Fast food and junk food marketing is big business. Food companies are willing to spend top dollar on advertising to capture their audience. Coke, Pepsi, McDonald's, Hardee's and the list goes on of the advertisers that spend billions each year to capture an audience. The price tag is worth it because the market is working – Americans spend $110 million on fast food in 2001 and consumed 56 gallons of soda per person that same year. In 2010 it was up to 200 million and 65 gallons.

An Old Problem Getting Worse

Many may think this health care crisis is new to the 21st century but it has been with us for quite some time. In 1988, C. Edward Koop, the Surgeon General of the United States, published a report stating that the America diet was the major cause of death in the United States.

In that report Koop states:

> "Although the precise proportion attributable to diet is uncertain, these nine conditions, coronary heart disease, cancer, stroke, diabetes, atherosclerosis, chronic lung disease, pneumonia, and influenza and chronic liver disease account for nearly 1.5 million of the 2.1 million total deaths in 1997. Dietary excesses and/or imbalances also contribute to other problems such as high blood pressure, obesity, dental disease, osteoporosis, and gastrointestinal diseases. Together, these diet-related conditions inflict a substantial burden of illness on American taxpayers."

In this same report, Koop listed some statistics of these diseases. Although the earlier numbers were alarming, the numbers today are staggering. For example:

Coronary Heart Disease (CHD): Causes nearly one quarter of all deaths in the United States. More than 600,000 deaths each year, one in every four deaths are attributed to heath disease. The cost was more than $304.6 billion in 2012.

Stroke: Stroke is another leading cause of death in the United States (about 130,000 people per year). The total cost of stroke to the American public is $43 billion per year and it is the leading cost of rehabilitation per year in the United States. If we had the time and the space we could give you much information on stroke since one of our authors was a victim of a brain hemorrhage from a Pheochromocytoma. Read the book he wrote in 2007 about the ravages of stroke in America, ***"A Stroke of Midnight"*** although the book sold several thousand copies. It was put on *Amazon.com* to him time to write another, *An Integrative Wellness Concept* you are reading now!

High Blood Pressure: Nearly 75 million people in the United States age 20 and older have high blood pressure.

Cancer: The cost of cancer is unbelievable in the Unites States. In 2006, there were more than 11,384,892 men and women living with cancer. The number of deaths was 559,312 that year at a cost of more than $72 billion.

Diabetes: 23.6 million people – 7.8% of the population have some form of diabetes, with a cost of more than $174 billion per year.

Obesity: In American alone there are more than 58 million people over weight, 40 million obese, and 3 million morbidly obese costing in excess of $75 billion each year for the American health consumer.

Osteoporosis: Today in the U.S. there are 10 million people projected to have the condition already and another 34 million estimated to have low bone mass, placing them at an increased risk of osteoporosis. In 2007, osteoporosis related fractures were responsible for assessed $19 billion in cost.

It is hard to believe that there are people dying of an inadequate diet in the United States where there is a surplus of food, but it's true. Plus, there appears to be diminished hope of reversing this trend despite Americans spending $1.4 trillion per year on health care.

The World Health Organization (WHO) ranked the U.S. number one in health care spending. But, even with this spending, the U.S. ranked well out of the top 10 in overall health status.

Five Wellness Stats You Should Know

If you ever wished you could boil down your most important wellness info to a few simple items, we've got the list for you right here! There are five numbers that strongly correlate with aging, heart disease, stroke, memory loss and sexual health, reports Michael Roizen, MD, chief wellness officer at the Cleveland Clinic. Here's what made his short list for optimum health and wellness.

1. *Blood Pressure* –ideal number 115/75 "blood pressure at this level lowers your risk of disability and premature death- plus it can help keep you feeling good and looking young." Dr. Roizen says.
2. *Cholesterol* – Ideal numbers: LDL (bad) cholesterol under 100; HDL (good) over 50. "Cholesterol at these levels is associated with healthy, youthful arteries."
3. *C-Reactive Protein* – Ideal number is less than 1. CRP rises when you have inflammation somewhere in your body- and chronic inflammation can mean trouble. A CRP below 1 will keep you at low risk of arthritis, heart disease, stroke and diabetes.
4. *HBA1c* – Ideal number: 5.6 or lower. This test measures glycated hemoglobin which is how much sugar is attached to your hemoglobin, an oxygen-carrying protein in the blood. The higher the number, the worse your blood sugar control and the more likely you are to develop diabetes or other sugar relate problems.
5. *Waist Circumference* – Ideal number: half or less of your height in inches. Wrap a tape measure around your middle at belly button level, and then suck in and measure. Any fat that you have in your belly is unlikely to cause disease or premature aging if your waist circumference is in check.

What's the Answer?

There are individuals who think modern medicine is the answer to the present health care crisis that keeps growing and threatening more each year. Modern Medicine is just not the answer and just not true and doesn't have to be the case. Using modern technology to cure disease is very expensive and often futile. Experts in the field of Public Health realize and admit the use of advanced technology has not decreased the health care crisis at all especially the cost.

The real answer does not rely on the cure of disease (look how long we have been fighting the common cold), but in the prevention of disease. One of the best ways of prevention is to boost your immune system and work toward a healthy lifestyle and wellness goal. For many people, understanding what constitutes the foundation of a healthy immune system is the same thing as a healthy lifestyle. This doesn't have to be difficult because it only consist of a few simple steps.

- *Eat healthy* – Kick the SAD system out of your life and replace it with a diet filled with fresh whole vegetables and fruit, whole grains and fresh meat and fish.
- *Work Out* – Exercising just 30 minutes three times per week will promote heart health, help you lose weight, increase your metabolism and boost your immune system.
- *Sleep Well* – Proper sleep allows your body to recharge and rebuild. Most cell repairs occur during sleep, as well as memory assimilation of the day's events important for mental and emotional balance.
- *Live Well* – Speaking of emotional health, kindness, love and respect for others, as well as having a set of principles to guide your life, will help you be healthier mentally and emotionally.
- *Seek Optimal Health and Wellness* – Everything that goes on in or around our body engages the ancient Chinese principle "Qi" and if it involves qi then the nervous system is implicated. Ridding your body of blockages and imbalances can help you reach your full potential.

Following these five simple steps can help you live a long healthy life without the usual complaints of aging.

This puts the burden for health squarely on your shoulders. You cannot rely on others to watch out for your health. You cannot find optimal health at the doctor's offices or in the pharmacy. You can't find it in the junk food aisles of the grocery store or in fast food restaurants. Good health can only be found within **you** through a healthy lifestyle and the ultimate goal of wellness.

In this country, modern medicine is used routinely for major surgeries such as bypasses and transplants. Seventy-five percent of health care costs are due to chronic diseases and only two percent are spent on prevention. To get healthy again, this will have to change and change begins with you.

By taking care of your body, mind and spirit now, learning everything you can about how to make good healthy choices, and finding practitioners that live and promote the prevention model of wellness you will be on the way to a happier, healthier and more harmonious life.

SUPPLEMENTS

Supplements aren't just for athletes or people wanting to "bulk up." Rather, they are to fill in the nutrient gaps that most people now experience thanks to the Standard American Diet (SAD). According to the National Health and Nutritional Examination survey (NHANES) – a program of studies designed to assess the health and nutritional status of adults and children in the United States… it turns out most Americans are nutrient deficient!

One of the most important things to understand these days is a concept called epigenetics, which is starting to be recognized by conventional medicine as well. "Epi" means 'above' in Latin. Contrary to previous beliefs, ours genes are not written in stone but rather are activated and affected by our environment. Epigenetics is the science that studies how environmental influences, such as diet, pollution, drugs, water, minerals, herbs and vitamins affect genes and turn them on or off to either help or hurt health and push the individual toward one side or the other of the Wellness Continuum.

One of nature's robust epigenetic molecules is vitamin D. Vitamin D is not really a vitamin but actually a type of hormone called *secosteriod hormone*, which acts similarly to steroids but with a slightly different structure. Only recently has science realized this. Because of its hormonal properties, vitamin D is now known to interact directly with more than 200 genes in the body. Vitamin D, when it's present in sufficient quantities, turns on and off these genes to help deliver better health.

Vitamin D deficiency is now linked to 17 different types of cancer. It is estimated that more than one billion people worldwide are deficient in vitamin D. Vitamin D deficiency during pregnancy and early childhood is linked with the triple epidemics of juvenile diabetes, childhood asthma and autism. Men with low levels of vitamin D have a 200 percent higher risk of heart problems than men with a normal level of vitamin D.

In one recent study, it was estimated that if every woman in America increased her levels of vitamin D, the incidence of breast cancer would be reduced by 50 percent. Women who had higher levels of vitamin D at the time of a diagnosis of breast cancer did significantly better over the ensuing ten years than women who had a lower vitamin D level at the time of diagnosis.

Normally our bodies obtain vitamin D from sunshine. However, too much sun is damaging to our skin, so using sunblock has been recommended for years. In fact, the sunblock that prevents skin cancer also impedes our ability to absorb vitamin D. This is one reason why we have such an epidemic of vitamin D deficiency in the western world. The amount of vitamin D that is added to products such as milk or found in fish, like mackerel, sardines, tuna, etc., does not in any way give one the desired levels of vitamin D we need in the body.

This is why in practice, we recommend everyone take Vitamin D every day, especially in the winter months when there is a tendency to get less sunlight. But getting your vitamin D from the sun can be tenacious business, because too much sun can obliviously damage the skin. There is an excellent book written by Soram Khalsa, MD, *The Vitamin D Revolution* which covers this in greater detail.

Of course other nutrients are important as well and you should not neglect the possibility of a deficiency just because you 'think' you eat well. Then again, one shouldn't assume a poor diet is made up for by taking supplements. Eating a nutritious diet, with some use of supplements is recommended. Foods today do not contain the nutrients they did in our grandparents day, 50 to 100 years ago. Let's look at some of the vitamins and supplements and talk about what they do and where they come from.

Vitamin A

It helps keep your vision and immune system healthy. One form of A (retinol) comes only from animal sources like fish and dairy. Another form comes from plants, most often beta-carotene (carrots and other orange colored fruits and vegetables are packed with it), which your body converts to the A that it needs. Getting a lot of A in your diet lowers the risk of lung cancer in your future.

How to Get It

Produce with orange, yellow and reddish flesh tends to be rich in vitamin A – sometimes really rich. For example, one baked sweet potato delivers 21,909 IU. The recommended daily allowance for women is 2,333 IU and for men 3,000 IU. Additional sources include:

- ½ cup carrots, raw (10,692 IU); about 5 times the daily need.
- ½ cup cantaloupe (2,706 IU)
- ½ cup red or yellow raw peppers (2,333 IU)
- Salmon, spinach, mangoes, black-eyed peas, apricots, and broccoli are all sources.

Vitamin A can build up in your body, but it's best to regularly eat a vitamin A rich diet.

Vitamin B

The B vitamins – there are eight individual types – are essential to core functions in the body, such as converting food to energy and maintaining your brain and nervous system. They are all important and generally easy to get in your diet, but two are particularly noteworthy: Folate or folic acid which is vitamin B9. This lowers the risk of birth defects such as spina bifida, which is why it's so critical that women who are pregnant or planning a family get enough of it. And vitamin B12 (cobalamin) helps to keep red blood cells, DNA, and your nervous system healthy.

How to Get Them

You'll get most of the B's easily from food. In America, all refined grains are fortified with folic acid (you need 400 mcg per day) and other B vitamins. Other sources of B's include meat, poultry, dairy products, fish, nuts, legumes, and many vegetables. B12 however is only found in animal products. You need 2.4 mcg per day and can get about half of that from a cup of 1% milk (.93mcg) or two hard-boiled eggs (1.11 mcg). If you're a vegan you'll need to take a supplement.

Supplement Tip

Your stomach absorbs less B12 from food as you age, so if you are over 50 consider a supplement. Aspirin and some heartburn medications (proton-pump inhibitors) may also leave your B12 low. Anemia and serious neurological problems can result from a B12 deficiency. As for folic acid, don't take any more than 1,000 mcg of it a day because large doses can mask symptoms of a B12 deficiency.

Vitamin C

Vitamin C is an antioxidant that helps your immune system fight disease. It doesn't prevent colds, but if you take it regularly, your colds more than likely will be shorter and less severe. It also contributes to collagen, which you need to heal wounds and build tissue. In addition, Vitamin C supplements have been linked to lower blood pressure.

How to Get It

It's easy to get vitamin C from food. The recommended daily allowance is 75 mg for women and 90 mg for men. Some food sources include:

- ½ cup of raw red pepper (95 mg)
- 1 cup orange juice (84 mg)
- 1 medium orange (70 mg)

Grapefruit, broccoli, strawberries, tomatoes, cantaloupe, and cauliflower are also good sources of C. Heat, light and air can destroy it, so eat vitamin C rich foods raw or lightly steamed.

Supplement Tip

Take a wholefood vitamin C supplement two or three times per day since C is water-soluble this keeps you from excreting the excess out in the urine.

Vitamin D has already been discussed so we'll go on to vitamin E.

Vitamin E

Vitamin E plays a big role in immunity and heart health. Getting this vitamin from food had been linked to a lower risk of heart disease.

How to Get It

The best sources of Vitamin E are nuts and oils, so if you avoid them you may be in trouble to get the recommended daily allowance of 15 mg or 22.4 IU. Some food sources include:

- 1 oz of almonds (6.8 mg)
- 1 cup cooked spinach (3.74 mg)
- 2 Tbsp peanut butter (2.9 mg)
- 1 Tbsp vegetable oil (2 mg)

Supplement Tip

Try to get most of your vitamin E from foods. If you do take a supplement, choose wholefood and be sure it contains mixed tocopherols.

Vitamin K

Vitamin K plays a big role in bone health and in making proteins necessary for blood to clot. Most people get about half the K they need from the food they eat in a form called K1. The rest comes mostly in K2, which is produced in by your body. Small amounts also come from meat and dairy.

How to Get It

If you eat leafy greens, you probably get the K1 you need. The recommended daily allowance is 90 mcg for women and 120 mcg for men. Food sources include:

- ½ cup cooked kale (531 mcg)
- ½ cup cooked collard greens (386 mcg)
- 1 cup raw spinach (145mcg)

Supplement Tip

It's advised that if you are on blood thinners, don't take vitamin K supplements without your doctor's knowledge. Also talk to your MD if you are taking antibiotics. Some of them can destroy the good bacteria in that body that make this vitamin.

General Recommendations

In an integrative wellness practice, doctors have very sophisticated tests to evaluate organ function in the "transitional gray zone" we discussed earlier. However, we realize not everyone can afford or wants to go to an integrative practitioner, because insurance often doesn't cover this type of preventive or wellness type of health care. We also realize a discipline of exercise, acupuncture, chiropractic, nutrition with diet changes and supplements may be too much for some people economically. Our intent is to show the individual the quickest route back to good balanced health and wellness. For this reason, we have several recommendations to minimize your risk of chronic degenerative disease.

In general, most if not all people should be following a wholefoods-eating program. This means avoiding processed foods to consume as few additives of chemicals as possible from cans, bottles or boxes. Take a good quality wholefood multivitamin, omega 3, vitamin D, and a probiotic like Zypan and Multizyme on a regular basis.

The omega 3 supplements are necessary because most people do not eat enough fish and seafood, while even farm raised animals like cattle no longer have enough omega 3 to meet human needs.

Vitamin D is important for our bones, skin and brain, as well as hormone creation and regulation. The probiotic is extremely helpful for digestion and the support of the body's immune system, as well as a healthy pH level in the digestive system. The probiotics help secrete metabolites with anti-inflammatory properties and much more for the gastrointestinal tract. Our digestive system contributes a major part of our immune system and should not be neglected.

Supplements can also be useful on a case-by–case basis to fill in specific nutrients that we are lacking in the diet or due to poor absorption. For example, some people will not eat kale, spinach or Brussels sprouts. It's recommend they take a *cruciferous* vegetable or green food supplement to ensure they are getting all the nutrients they need.

There are hundreds of supplements on the market, some better than others. You have a wide variety to select from. One can get lost in the scheme of things when it comes to supplements of vitamins, minerals, enzymes and herbals. There are certain criteria that you should be aware of before selecting your supplements.

The first consideration should be natural versus synthetic. Natural is better but does tend to be more expensive. Before you decide, ask yourself why are you going to take these supplements, if the answer is an affirmative determined desire to be fit, healthy and live a wellness lifestyle you should select the natural category? We recommend you buy natural unless synthetic supplements are the only ones you can afford to buy. Synthetic supplements are better than nothing! Also, find a health food store that sells high quality natural supplements and the quantity sufficient to make you feel like you are not being swindled.

When asking a number of colleagues where they order their supplements from and why, we found that the clear majority readily agreed there was a gold standard to meet with natural supplements set by *Standard Process Company* of Palmyra, Wisconsin (www.standardprocess.com). They have been in business for over 100 years as one of the few whole food supplement-manufacturing companies in the United States. This is the company many nutrition professors and contemporaries in Integrative practices recommend. For herbs, the Medi-Herb Company out of Australia, which deals only high quality herbs, is recommended.

HERBS

Our lead author has a special place in his heart for herbs and natural supplements in general because of his grandmother's practice. As a young boy around ten, he would go with her into the mountains of West Virginia, Kentucky and Tennessee to gather special herbs. She would walk, talk and teach him how to identify the herbs and what they were good for, as well as how they should be used with certain conditions.

For example, there is an herb that could be called nature's Prozac. This is good news for those with mild depression, or winter doldrums. A study published in *Phytotherapy Research,* whose author Ajay Goel, PhD is director of epigenetics and cancer prevention at Baylor University, found curcumin to be effective in treating depression. Dr Goel said "We studied the effects of curcumin on patients with major depressive disorders." They found that 1000 mg daily of curcumin – an active compound in the herb turmeric – proved to be just as effective at treating depression as fluoxetine, the antidepressant better known as Prozac. Curcumin inhibits the production of monoamine oxidase, an enzyme that at high levels is linked to depression. In addition the herb has good anti-inflammatory properties.

There are many such scientific notations that could be made about herbs but suffice it to say herbs are safe and easily used the world over for minor aches, pains and other health conditions.

This leads us into another area that many practitioners use and practice quite extensively ***Homeopathy*** and ***Naturopathy***.

Chapter VIII

HOMEOPATHY AND NATUROPATHY

"A human being is part of the whole, called by us 'Universe,' a part limited in time and space. He experiences himself, his thoughts and feelings as something separated from the rest – a kind of optical delusion of his consciousness. This delusion is a kind of prison for us, restricting us to our personal desires and to affection for a few persons nearest to us. Our task must be to free ourselves from this prison by widening our circle of compassion to embrace all living creatures and the whole of nature in its beauty. Nobody is able to achieve this completely, but striving for such achievement is in itself part of the liberation and a foundation for inner security."

ALBERT EINSTEIN (1879-1955)

HOMEOPATHY

Homeopathy is a type of alternative medicine that goes back to 1796 when it was developed by a physician called Samuel Hahnemann. It is based on the concept of "like cures like." Here a substance that would cause symptoms of a disease in healthy people, is used in small doses to treat people with that disease. He investigated a claim that cinchona, the bark of a Peruvian tree, was effective in treating malaria. He tested the effect of cinchona on a healthy person via self-application, and found that he experienced malaria like symptoms. This led to his principle of "like cures like" for which he coined the term "homeopathy." This law of cure has been verified by millions of homoeopaths all over the world since the time of Hahnemann. This principle is seen in modern medicine by the use of allergens in allergy desensitization shots, viruses in vaccines, plus using medications like Ritalin to treat hyperactivity.

Hahnemann is called the Father of Experimental Pharmacology because he studied the effects of substances on both healthy and sick individuals. Before Hahnemann, medicines were given on a speculative basis without experimental verification. Dr. Hahnemann discovered the remedial powers of drugs and inert substances such as gold, platinum, silica, vegetable charcoal, lycopodium, etc. By preparing the medicines through potentization, these inert and insoluble substances became soluble in alcohol or water and were charged with an energetic force.

It was at that time in history he described and promoted vital force or life force, a force that was closely linked to the constitutional strength of the body and its ability to overcome illness. Vital force is the philosophy of energy of life, a holistic concept.

This holistic energy medicine addresses all aspects of a person; body, mind and spirit."

Homeopathic medicine is created by taking a small amount of a substance and creating a highly diluted solution in water, along with vigorous successions (shaking), to transfer the energy of the medicinal substance into the water.

The successions (also called potentization) create an energetic imprint of the original substance in the water. This imprint is enough to gently stimulate the body to overcome the symptoms of an illness, but not enough to cause any negative side effects form the formula.

Homeopathy even though practiced by many natural practitioners today can also be used by the layman with no training or expertise. Like self-medication, we want to caution against this type of use of homeopathic tinctures and cures. Even though the tincture may not be harmful, it may delay the treatment of a serious illness or condition. We suggest seeking the advice of a licensed health care provider before going on homeopathic medicines for an extended period.

This is not to say that either Homeopathy or Naturopathy aren't capable of getting the same results as herbs, vitamins, enzymes or minerals get when used with an illness or condition. One must be careful and we suggest the most conservative medication for an illness, injury or condition first, before going on to a more dangerous prescription. This is why we often try herbs, homeopathic and naturopathic approaches first.

NATUROPATHY

This is a fairly broad term in that Naturopathy includes a wide array of "natural" treatments, including homeopathy, herbalism, and acupuncture, as well as diet and lifestyle counseling. Naturopaths favor a holistic approach with non-invasive treatment and generally avoid the use of surgery and drugs. Naturopathic philosophy is based on a belief in vitalism and self-healing, and practitioners often prefer methods of treatment that are not compatible with evidence-based medicine. In the opinion of modern medicine, naturopathic medicine is replete with pseudoscientific, ineffective, unethical, and possibly dangerous practices.

Modern naturopathy grew out of the Natural Cure movement of Europe. The term was coined in 1895 by John Scheel and popularized by Benedict Lust, the "father of U.S. naturopathy." Beginning in the 1970s, there was a revival of interest in the United States and Canada, in conjunction with the holistic health movement. Today, naturopathy is primarily practiced in the United States and Canada.

The term "Naturopathic Doctor (ND)" does not necessarily imply a specific educational background, as this term is licensed in only some states. Those who call themselves Naturopathic Doctors can be one of three types.

1) Medical doctors who employ the principles of naturopathy.
2) Traditional Naturopaths who are not physicians. Education and training varies and licensing differs by state. They deal with lifestyle changes and not diagnosing or treating disease.
3) Other health care providers that provide naturopathic services.

Much of the ideology and methodological underpinnings of naturopathy are in conflict with the paradigm of evidence-based medicine. Many naturopaths oppose vaccination based in part on the early views that shaped the profession. According to the American Cancer Society, "scientific evidence does not support claims that naturopathic medicine can cure cancer or any other disease, since virtually no studies on naturopathy as a whole have been published."

In our practice we use vitamins, minerals, enzymes, herbs and tintures to help restore the human body back to where it should be when dealing with conditions such as: alopecia (patchy hair loss), digestion problems, arthritis, gout, sinusitis, colds, flu, and many other conditions. When these natural formulas go longer than 30 days or four weeks without showing some help or progress then it may be time to consider medical intervention for the condition, but naturopathy still should be an alternative people have a right to select from when considering their health care needs.

Natural Ways to Break Bad Habits

Here are some useful "tricks" that are a natural and drug free way to help modify behavior in positive ways.

Mind Tricks To Help You Break Bad Habits

1. Avoid negative self-talk

Complaining can quickly drain your motivation. Instead of thinking, “This is so hard,” or “What’s the point?” substitute more empowering ones: “It’s hard but not impossible.” “Hang in there. It will be easier tomorrow.” “I won’t be sorry I struck to it.”

2. Reframe discomfort as a positive

Feeling uncomfortable is a sign that you are making progress toward change, and tolerating the discomfort will make you mentally stronger – not just for the habit you are working to change, but also other challenges in your life.

3. Distract yourself for 15 minutes

Take a walk; answer emails; do a small task that you have been putting off (bonus benefit). Focus your mind on something other than dwelling on what your emotional urges are telling you what to do. After 15 minutes the craving should subside.

4. Does progress seem slow?

Focus on small units. If you've struggled to go three days without a cigarette, it's hard to imagine how you'll make it through the first month, let alone the rest of your life. Instead, focus on how far you've come, and set a more short-term goal: "Three days done. One more and I'll be more than halfway through the week.

5. Forgive your slipups

Everyone has lapses. Understand what happened and learn from it and get back to the program the next day.

6. Feeling discouraged?

Don't have the motivation to continue? No need to make a decision today. Reread #1 and #2 above, and sleep on it.

Chapter IX

THE HUMAN TOUCH

"I promise myself…
To be so strong that nothing can disturb my peace of mind.
To talk health, happiness, and prosperity to every person I meet.
To make all my friends feel that there is something worthwhile in them.
To look at the sunny side of everything and make my optimism come true.
To think only of the best, to work only for the best, and expect only the best.
To be just as enthusiastic about the success of others as I am about my own."

CHRISTIAN LARSON (1874-1954)

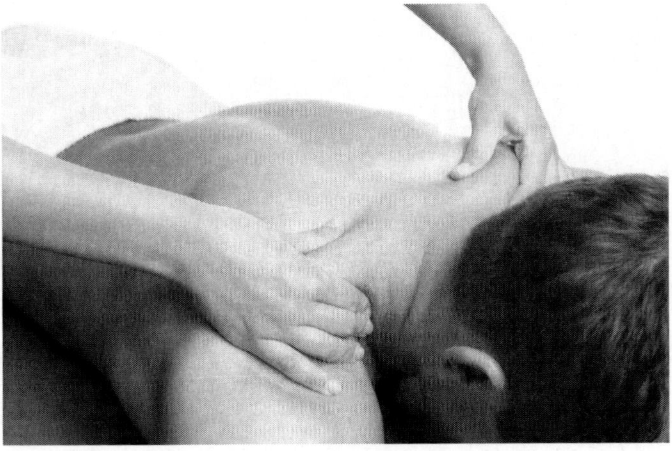

MASSAGE THERAPY

Massage therapy is an integral part of our health and wellness plan. Massage can be defined as the systematic manual or mechanical manipulation of the soft tissues of the body by such movements of the body as rubbing, kneading, rolling, pressing, slapping and tapping for therapeutic purposes. Massage is conducted for the purpose of promoting circulation of the blood and lymph, relaxation of muscles, relief from pain, restoration of metabolic balance, and other such benefits both mental and physical.

The massage practitioner has been referred to by several titles such as massage technician or massotherapist. In the past, a male massage practitioner may have been called a masseur (ma-sur), and a female practitioner a masseuse (ma-soos). Today, most professionally trained men and women prefer to be called *massage practitioners* or *massage therapists.* For practical purposes, massage therapist is the term we will use in this book.

Massage has been a major part of Eastern medicine and health care for at least 5,000 years and important in Western medicine for at least 3,000 years. Massage was practiced, developed and taught primarily by physicians and practitioners. It has been written about extensively in medical texts since 500 B.C. and was a major topic in the first medical text printed after the discovery of the printing press. An entire book could be written on this subject and thousands have been over the years. One contemporary author that we have worked closely with a number of years is Donna Kyle-Brown, the author of *Therapeutic Massage and Bodywork*, published by McGraw-Hill, 2008. This is a great reference book for any serious Massage specialist.

There are many different types of massage and techniques within the profession. Let's look at a few:

CHINESE ANMO

In the British museum of history, records reveal that as early as 3000 B.C., the Chinese practiced and kept records of massage benefits. The *Gong Fou* of Tao-Tse was one of the ancient Chinese books that described the use of medicinal plants, exercises and a system of body massage for the treatment of disease and the maintenance of health. The Chinese continued to improve the massage techniques through a special procedure they called ***Anmo.*** This massage technique was developed over centuries in finding the points on the body where various movements such as rubbing, pressing and manipulations of soft tissue where most effective.

Today, the use of massage is an integral part of Chinese health care and is practiced in medical clinics and hospitals. A more modern term for Chinese message is called ***tui-na***, and literally means, “push-pull” of the body’s soft tissues.

JAPANESE TSUBO AND SHIATSU

The practice of the Anmo method of massage entered Japan about the sixth century A.D. The points of stimulation remained much the same as the Chinese points but were called ***tsubo***. These points are pressed to effect circulation of fluids and Qi (life force or energy) and stimulate nerves with a finger pressure procedure called Japanese ***Shiatsu.*** This massage technique has become quite popular in recent years. Early records show that a book on massage, The *San-Tsai-Tou-Hoei,* was published in Japan in the sixteenth century and listed both active (yang) and passive (yin) massage techniques. One of the books used in Japan was called *Zen Shiatsu, as taught by Shizuto Masunago and Wataru Ohashi.* They are credited with establishing the scientific basis for the practice in both Japan and America.

TODAY’S MASSAGE

We could continue to name and describe the massage techniques throughout the world that are an accepted part of the medical arts of each country today. Modern massage terminology is credited to Dr. Johann Mezger (1839-1909) of Holland, who established the practice and art of massage as a scientific subject for physicians in the remedial treatment of disease. Through Mezger’s efforts massage became recognized as fundamental to rehabilitation in physical therapy.

Beginning around 1960, a massage renaissance began to take place in the United States. The development of the wellness model, places more emphasis on prevention and recognizes the importance of controlling stress and advocates the use of massage and bodywork. The psychological benefits of touch and its proven use in the treatment of pain returned massage to a place of prominence in the health care system.

There is Sports massage, Rolfing and massage, Thai, Reflexology, Touch for Health, Neuromuscular techniques, and Craniosacral therapy, all in the realm of massage therapy. Many Massage Therapists in Wellness Centers use the majority of these techniques in practice.

If you feel that massage will help with your problem mention this to the treating doctor or therapist and make arrangements to work this into your treatment schedule.

Chapter X

INTEGRATIVE MEDICINE

"It's not what happens to you, but how you react that matters."

EPICTETUS (c. AD 55-c. 135)

MEDICAL INTERVENTION

When Integrative Medicine is the topic it's a slippery slope. First, not many practitioners of allopathic medicine want to practice natural medicine because it's too slow and the results are not as dramatic as allopathic medicine. That being said, too many physicians today primarily practice a form of applied pharmacology: if this Rx doesn't work, we'll try another and another. Back in the old days physicians were taught to investigate the condition and illness to see if the person with the illness had something wrong that would cause the condition to develop. Now there is very little investigation except by the diagnostician or the MD in charge of the case and in charge of eventually making the diagnosis. Sometimes this could take days, weeks or months waiting for test, labs and more tests.

Physicians today do not want to wait to allow the body to heal itself, as it is capable of doing in 90% of the illnesses that develop. They jump in with a barrage of medications that usually lower the immune system and complicate the case. We feel that medical intervention should be brought in, but not first, when an illness develops. Usually there's an underlying reason you have become sick and it is the physician's job to find what the reason is and try to correct the cause. Medication is good at covering up the symptoms and hiding the cause of the real disease but most people would like to correct the underlying source of the problem.

Physicians are so busy today trying to patch up the sick with medications and surgery they forget to ask the real questions at the basis of many very sick and ill patients. We shouldn't accept the idea of self-healing as automatic and spontaneous. To say you can heal yourself is sort of a misnomer because scientific evidence concludes that the role of the healer is essential. But even then we should take advantage of the miracles of modern medicine but not depend on it exclusively. It's important to get to the root cause of why you might be sick or injured in the first place. What predisposed that cancer to grow? Why were you susceptible to that infection, when others probably many others exposed at the same time? What in your life might be causing this chronic pain for the last five years? These are some of the questions you and your physician should seek answers to.

DIAGNOSIS

When a sick patient visits a doctor, diagnosis is the first step. Physicians should begin forming some type of diagnosis from the time they examine a patient because that's the way medical training works. The physician will form some kind of opinion based on experience and training, and the patient's symptoms and story. If a patient is moving well and talking clearly, it's unlikely they are experiencing a stroke. That's a quick first diagnosis. Then the doctor forms what's called a differential diagnosis, a list of all the possible diseases/conditions the patient could possibly have. If the patient keeps talking and the physician does an examination or further testing, they narrow down that differential diagnosis until reaching the most likely explanation of the patient's condition. Every physician goes through that same sequence of training for diagnosis, even the Chiropractic physician. The doctor knows or has an idea of what is happening, so don't leave their office until you have something even if it's their working diagnosis.

Always tell the doctor everything, the whole story. The majority of diagnoses can be made on a patient's story and symptoms during a consult. If you hold something back, the doctor might not reach the proper conclusion. Telling the complete story is part of the "Eight pillars to a better diagnosis." Referred to in the book: *"When Doctors Don't Listen: How to Avoid Misdiagnoses and Unnecessary Test."* By Leana Wen, MD who is a Rhodes Scholar and attending Physician and Director of Patient Centered Care

Research in the Department of Emergency Medicine at George Washington University Hospital in Washington D.C.

There is much we could add about a proper diagnosis but remember you are as responsible as the physician for reaching the complete and proper diagnosis. If you give the false, incomplete or wrong information that is usually what they have to base the diagnosis on at least in the beginning.

INFLAMMATION

Many scientist and doctors worldwide have come to the same conclusion after reviewing thousands of studies and ground breaking new research on disease and aging. It is now understood that perhaps all chronic diseases including aging have the same trigger… inflammation!

Short-term inflammation is actually beneficial and is the body's short-term response to infection or injury. This has the constructive effect of ending the infection or speeding repair of the injury. However, long-term chronic inflammation (called metaflammation) is another matter entirely. An article published in *Preventing Chronic Disease* stated "The discovery of a form of low-grade systemic and chronic inflammation ("metaflammation"), linked to inducers (broadly termed "anthropogens") associated with modern man-made environments and lifestyles, suggests an underlying basis for chronic disease that could provide a 21st-century equivalent of the germ theory." (Egger, 2012) These inducers or "anthropogens" of inflammation will be covered below.

The United States Center for Disease Control and Prevention, commonly referred to as the CDC, listed the top ten causes of mortality in the US in 2013 as follows:

Number of Deaths for Leading Causes (CDC, 2013)

- Heart disease: 611,105
- Cancer: 584,881
- Chronic lower respiratory diseases: 149,205
- Stroke (cerebrovascular diseases): 128,978
- Accidents (unintentional injuries): 130,557
- Alzheimer's disease: 84,767

- Diabetes: 75,578
- Influenza and Pneumonia: 56,979
- Nephritis, nephrotic syndrome, and nephrosis: 47,112
- Intentional self-harm (suicide): 41,149

All of these but three (accidents, flu/pneumonia, and suicide) are linked to chronic inflammation. These are the diseases of modern society in developed countries.

Things That Increase Chronic Inflammation (Anthropogens)

- *Being overweight*
  Fat cells produce extra inflammatory chemicals in the body.
- *Smoking*
- *Sugar*
  Foods high in sugar raise the blood sugar level which leads to the body generating more free radicals. Free radicals in turn inflame the lining of blood vessels.
- *Processed white flour*
  The body quickly converts processed white flour into sugar.
- *Tran fats*
  Foods that are fried in or made with partially hydrogenated vegetable oils contain trans fats which are linked to inflammation.
- *Fried Foods*
  Frying foods requires very high temperatures, which creates a chemical called acrylamide. Acrylamide is known to contribute to inflammation.
- *Nitrates*
  Nitrates are found in bacon, processed lunch meat, and sausage. These are known cancer-causing chemicals that trigger inflammation.
- *Alcohol*
  The Mayo Clinic and other research based institutes have found that inflammatory markers are very high when alcohol is consumed verses not. However, it should be noted that some research has shown that moderate intake of some alcohol can be beneficial.

- *Soda*

  Soda contains either sugar or synthetic sweeteners like aspartame. Both increase inflammation.
- *Additives/food coloring/preservatives*

  Additives/food coloring/preservatives cause oxidative damage to your cells. These free radicals from these chemicals tear at our cells causing inflammation.
- *Lack of Sleep*

  Losing sleep for even one night can trigger the key cellular pathway that produces tissue-damaging inflammation.
- *Stress*

  Chronic stress changes gene activity of immune cells before they enter the blood stream leading to increased inflammation.

Foods and Behaviors that Fight Inflammation

- *Fruits and Vegetables*

  Many fruits and vegetables are high in antioxidants, which decrease free radicals and inflammation. Color is a good indicator of the antioxidant level. Dark green and orange, yellow and red are good bets. Dark green includes spinach, broccoli, kale, brussel sprouts, avocadoes, etc. Orange, yellow and red include carrots, melons, citrus fruit, cranberries, peppers, sweet potatoes, squash, berries, etc.. Eating more fruits and vegetables will also increase your fiber consumption. Fiber also decreases inflammation.
- *Fish high in Omega-3*

  This includes salmon, herring, mackerel, sardines and anchovies. These fish contain healthy monosaturated fats and are high in omega-3 fatty acids, both of which reduce inflammation.
- *Extra Virgin Olive Oil*

  Extra Virgin olive oil has a rich supply of polyphenols that protect the heart and blood vessels from inflammation. Olive oil is the juice of a fruit, so fresher is better. Check for the harvest date.
- *Raw Nuts*

  Nuts contain specific fatty acids that squelch the inflammatory fires that rage in the body at times. Almonds, Walnuts and Pecans are a rich source of fatty acids that create two omega-3 fatty acids that help quiet the inflammation. Flax seeds, Macadamia nuts, Hazelnuts and Pistachios (non-colored shell) are great choices also.

- *Herbs & Spices*

  There are a number of herbs and spices that show extremely good anti-inflammatory benefits. Green Tea contains a natural anti-oxidant called epigallocatechin-3 gallate (ECCG) not found in black tea that stops the production of certain inflammatory chemicals in the body. Turmeric, Cinnamon, Garlic, Basil, Oregano and Ginger are some of the preferences because they diminish inflammation and have scientific studies stipulating evidence.
- *Dark Chocolate*

  Here is good news for chocolate lovers. Cocoa comes from the cocoa bean that is the fruit of the cocoa tree. So depending on how you look at it, cocoa can be considered both a fruit and a vegetable. Cocoa is full of nutrients and antioxidants. To be healthy, dark chocolate should be high in cocoa content and low in sugar content. Not the sweet stuff! Unsweetened baking chocolate is 100% cocoa, but is very bitter. Dark chocolate that is around 70% cocoa is a more palatable choice.
- *Adequate Sleep*

  Getting 7-8 hours of good sleep each night reduces inflammation.
- *Exercise and Stretching*

  While over doing exercise can cause inflammation, in the long run a program of regular exercises and stretching will reduce inflammation.

Chronic low-grade inflammation is a ‘silent killer’ with thousands of research studies to support this position. Cellular inflammation either causes or seriously increases disease and aging in the body. We can reduce this possibility of disease and aging by following the proper lifestyle, with the focus on good nutritional habits, proper routine exercise, happy attitude and good thoughts!

Human Growth Hormone (hGH)

Do you want to reduce body fat, increase lean muscle mass, boost mood, heighten sex drive, have plenty of energy, and get rid of wrinkles and love handles, look and feel decades younger? If you said no, we don't believe you! But you'll pay and pay big. Celebrities, CEOs, Wall Street executives, models, athletes and many others are drinking the Kool-Aid. There's no doubt about it; in our fast paced, youth oriented culture, human growth hormone (hGH) is a hot commodity.

The controversy isn't over whether or not hGH plays an essential role in our health and aging, virtually everyone agrees on that. Instead, the debate lies in the best way to maintain our body's supply of human growth hormone. Until recently, most felt the best way was through expensive prescription injections (cost can run as high as $1,500 per month). However, many physicians argue against injecting synthetic hGH in the body, because these synthetic hormones may interfere with the body's natural hGH production. Some have even stated the synthetic injections can cause cancer in the endocrine system. Because of these concerns researchers have spent the last 30 years searching for a reliable, clinically proven way to promote pituitary health, thereby increasing human growth hormone naturally. They are now capable of putting hGH in a capsule in order not to have to subject the body to dose after dose of the synthetic formula and subject the patient to possible cancer. This is simply one way in which MD's are trying to work in the Integrative Wellness and Prevention market and are doing a very good job.

We Can Do Something About Poor Wellness Habits

One of the 'biggest' wellness issues in the United States today is poor nutrition and related poor health habits. It has become a primary health concern with excess weight now becoming a disease classification. Integrative wellness has several weight loss methods you may wish to select from before trying prescriptions when dealing with this chronic issue. We would like to see a person keep their body mass index (BMI) under 25. You can ask your doctor what this involves but simply put this is how your height and weight match up.

Also, Acupuncture has a method of placing ear tacs on the ear in certain locations to stimulate the hypothalamic reflex and decrease hunger and desire for food. This method takes about one month and dietary restrictions must be followed during this time.

There is also the TMA (Trace Mineral Analysis) method of analysis to see if there is a deficiency in the body caused by certain mineral imbalances that can be determined with a hair sample. If there is an adrenal and thyroid imbalance, this can be corrected, allowing weight loss to begin.

In either method you choose, there is no magic bullet and certain dietary and lifestyle changes must be made including diet and exercise. Each person is different and will follow an individualized program for at least 4 months before a final analysis can be made.

Talk to your practitioner to determine if either of these is a method you wish to use for your weight reduction. In some instances, a patient who is pre-diabetic or a diagnosed Type II diabetic, he or she should and/or must be under medical management. Most Physicians will work with your Integrative practitioner to reach a good weight management plan and goal.

Chapter XI

WELLNESS FOR THE SENIORS AS THEY AGE

"Think of all the beauty still left around you and be happy."

ANNE FRANK (1929-1945)

Seniors (those 60 and older) experience changes in their health as they age. Some of these changes can be quite dramatic. That is why care by an Integrative practitioner can be so important during this critical time of life. At one time, one of the most feared of all senior's conditions was that of stroke. Today that view has changed. Now, middle-aged people and younger are having strokes at an alarming rate. It is happening to such a degree we were not sure if we should include this information in the senior section or made it a separate section all together.

SIMPLE STROKE PREVENTION TIPS

The consequences of stroke, also called brain attack, can be devastating: cognitive impairment, paralysis even death. A stroke can occur as a result of bleeding in the brain (hemorrhagic stroke) or blocked blood flow to the brain (ischemic stroke). The longer the blood supply is blocked, the more brain cells are destroyed – and the greater the physical and cognitive damage (Read "A Stroke of Midnight" *Amazon.com "Kindle"* by John and Dianne Stump).

"Just 30 minutes of physical activity, five or six days each week, can significantly lower your risk of stroke, heart disease, and diabetes."

Dr. John Stump

Each year, about 795,000 people in the United States suffer a stroke. It's our nation's number four killer and the leading cause of long-term disability. Yet most of the population is regrettably ignorant about the risk factors for stroke. The medical profession and the media have been relatively successful in educating the public about heart attacks, diabetes, cancer, and HIV, but stroke has received much less attention.

What's more, the real disappointing fact is, 80 percent of all strokes are preventable, according to the American Stroke Association (ASA). To help combat these alarming statistics, the ASA and the American Heart Association (AHA) joined forces to create Life's Simple Seven. This quick risk assessment and prevention tool focuses on seven ways to prevent stroke:

- Getting active
- Eating better
- Losing weight
- Managing blood pressure
- Controlling cholesterol
- Reducing blood sugar
- Don't smoke

Go to *mylifecheck.org,* plug in a few numbers along with a few lifestyle habits and you can calculate your risk. In a nationwide study of more than 20,000 adults published in the medical journal *Circulation,* people who met just one of the prevention criteria identified by Life's Simple Seven had a 25 percent reduction in stroke risk.

Life's Simple Seven reaffirms the accepted wisdom that what's good for the heart is good for the brain. While stroke undoubtedly has a strong genetic link, four of the seven 'Life's Simple Seven' are lifestyle related. If we would start by getting our behaviors in restraint, we may not need medications to control the other three factors (blood pressure, blood glucose, and cholesterol).

Investing in your health and wellness, whether by increasing physical activity or eating better, can translate into more successful aging. It may even help you live into your golden years free of heart disease, cancer, stroke or dementia to say nothing of its impact on your quality of life. As we age isn't that what we all want?

What Changes as Seniors Age

Disc, joints, ligaments, muscles and other tissues become weaker, less hydrated, more fibrotic and less able to withstand normal daily stresses. All of these issues can lead to arthritis, which the most common senior symptom and complaint. *Arthritis* is inflammation in one or more joints that results in pain, swelling, stiffness and limited movement.

Additionally, seniors are more likely to have tissue injury and face an increase in recuperation time from these injuries. Seniors see these injuries often occur due to everyday events such as bending, lifting or climbing stairs.

Integrative wellness practitioners understand the progress of aging as it relates to the whole body and can provide an effective, safe and non-invasive treatment plan. You may wish to start with either service you feel the need for. However, if you need evaluation and consultation before being referred to a service we will be happy to schedule this as well. The pain may be great, the fatigue severe and you might not know where to start. The Integrative wellness practitioner can evaluate your case and get you to the right practitioner to correct the problems.

Goals of Senior Care

Just as with others, a senior's care will depend on the individuals need. In addition to the severity of the condition, a look at the overall health of the individual is invaluable. Integrative health and wellness will look at the overall condition of the patient. Individuals that are in good overall health and still maintain an active lifestyle will find that their treatments are much more effective. It is known that acupuncture; chiropractic, massage, homeopathy and osteopathy plus some of the other mentioned techniques help different types of pain. When you add the proper nutrition, exercise and lifestyle you have a complete gamut of health and wellness. This will allow any senior to enjoy all the activities appreciated before their condition occurred.

Depending upon the overall health and activity of the patient, wellness goals can be one or more of the following:

1) Return to an active lifestyle with no pain
2) Return to an active lifestyle with some limitations
3) Return to some activities with some pain
4) Slow down the degenerative process

Although there is significant difference between these goals, even with the fourth goal the objective and result will be a step up from a degenerative disease with constant pain and practically no lifestyle.

Benefits of Senior Care

Many seniors are unaware of the remarkable results that are possible through the natural therapeutic care received at an Integrative Wellness practice. Because they are not familiar with the terms and procedures they equate it to a medical practice. Even though it looks the same in many ways the approaches are very different.

Pain Relief

Chiropractic and Acupuncture are probably the top two non-pharmaceutical therapeutic procedures used today for pain. Both Acupuncturists and Chiropractors are especially trained to identify and treat the imbalances and impairments found in the individual. Only when there is no other alternative are drugs or surgery recommended. However, with that being said, we have seen thousands of cases where a patient with a chronic condition like arthritis was receiving various pain medications for many years, switching from one prescription to another without sufficient relief. People often feel they have no other alternatives, but there are alternatives to be found in *Alternative* Medicine that can provide relief for many.

Increased Range of Motion

Seniors often experience a loss of range of motion throughout the years. As we age, muscles become shorter and lose their elasticity. This can be exacerbated by lack of use and poor nutrition. Additionally, ageing can affect the structure of bones, muscles and other tissues, causing pain and decreased range of motion in the fingers, wrist, shoulders, hips, knees and spine. Decreased range of motion can also come about from causes such as arthritis, Parkinson's disease, overuse syndromes from previous occupations, auto accidents, as well as falls. All of these can decrease range of motion, and increase muscle spasms and pain.

A decreased range of motion is something that no one wants. Regardless of the activity a person participates in, the range of motion is one of the body's most important components of fitness. As one ages, you want to be able to interact with the people around you, especially your family. You want to be able to bend down and pick up your grandchildren and you can do it better and more easily with a full range of motion. Maybe you are a golfer, bowler or a shuffle board player and want a better range of motion and more strength to improve your game. Whatever your endeavor and activity it will be improved with a better range of motion!

The goal is to improve your range of motion without jeopardy to your body without injury, strain or pain. In the Far East you find many seniors and elderly individuals well into their 90's still working out daily. However, the workouts do not involve fast or high impact movements like Pilates or Aerobics do. In East one finds seniors gathered in groups of 25 or so doing Tai Qi or Qigong, which are forms of exercise that concentrate the physical movement pattern on the function of the joints and muscles of the body without stress.

The forms take you through a series of slow flowing movements that allow the body to shift and glide effortlessly from one position to the other. At the end of the 20-minute session you have had a very complete workout without stress or strain to the body.

Then there is another discipline called Yoga that is very old and originated in India that is practiced all over the world today. The original essence of this discipline was basically spiritual but today is practiced all over the world with different emphasis. Many people today are not so interested in the spiritual discipline as they are the physical essence of the Yoga technique and choose to practice a purely physical type of Yoga that concentrates on stretching, pulling, pushing and breathing techniques that keep the joints, ligaments, tendons and muscles engaged and healthy without stress or strain to the physical body.

Increased Balance and Coordination

A loss of balance and coordination in seniors usually comes from a previous injury, degenerative changes or inner ear problems. Mechanoreceptors located in the cervical joints of the neck are responsible for proving the brain with information needed for balance and coordination. These work by telling the brain where the head is in relation to the body at any given time. Gradual aging causes minor deficiencies in the body's mechanoreceptors' function and results in a loss in body awareness. Then instead of using the mechanoreceptors, a person may have to rely only vision to determine where they are in space.

To compensate for the loss of awareness or location, the feet are kept wider apart than normal, causing a change in gait, resulting in musculoskeletal problems. As impairment increases, compensation becomes more difficult until finally, the senior is unable to get up from a chair or rise from a slip or fall. A huge population of seniors experience a pain syndrome and other problems following a fall. According to the Center for Disease Control and Prevention (CDC), falls are responsible for 90% of the 850,000 bone fractures each year among seniors 65 and older.

Integrative wellness practitioners use chiropractic, massage, acupuncture and osteopathic procedures to stimulate the mechanoreceptors, leading to improved balance and coordination, reducing the likelihood of falls.

Tissue Degeneration in Aging

When your body has a malposition, imbalance or subluxation, problems may occur. Think of this imbalance like you would a misalignment of the tires on your vehicle. Having your tires misaligned causes them to wear out faster and usually more on one side or the other. The same is true with your body imbalances and misalignments.

Integrative practitioners are specifically trained to determine if you have a mechanical or a physiological imbalance in need of correction. Chiropractors are trained to approach the body from mechanical or structural methodology. The Acupuncturist is trained more from a physiological or functional basis. Neither is right or wrong. Which is better depends on the individual patient. Sometimes it takes the combination to correct a problem.

Let's discuss some specifics of the tissue degeneration topic. Arthritis literally means joint inflammation. Arthritis causes pain, loss of movement and sometimes edema (swelling). Osteoarthritis (OA) is the most common type of arthritis in the senior population. It starts when connective tissue, called cartilage begins to wear and tear easily causing the bones to be exposed to irritation and inflammation. The cartilage acts as a cushion or pad for your joints. OA most often happens in your hands, neck, lower back, knees and feet. You notice these are the weight-being joints of the body in most cases.

After a while, OA can make it hard to move your joints, it can cause disability and dysfunction to the joints involved. Determining the cause of arthritis can be difficult, because often there are several contributory factors involved. Some of the risk factors that can contribute to OA include:

1) Genetics
2) Age
3) Weight
4) Previous activity
5) Occupational involvement
6) Sports and activity
7) Illness and infection
8) Poor nutrition

Aging seems to be the most common factor involved. This is because your joints and the connective tissue around them become less able to accommodate the changes and stresses of the daily activity involved.

The cartilage and connective tissue need the correct nutrition to repair and withstand the precise repair dynamics and also for the body to be able to remove cell waste and debris and heal properly. This happens through a decreased inflammatory reaction, proper joint movement and the proper nutrition in the body. A treatment plan for arthritis would involve stopping the inflammatory reaction, restoring joint mobility and minimizing the degenerative joint changes that have occurred over time.

At this stage many patients ask if their insurance pays for their maintenance care. Unfortunately few insurance companies are advanced enough in their planning or thinking to understand the benefits of prevention, maintenance and wellness health care, if they did our health care system would not be in the condition it is today. However, techniques and procedures like Chiropractic care pay some benefits through insurance and Medicare. Please check with your Integrative practitioner and health care provider to ask about specifics.

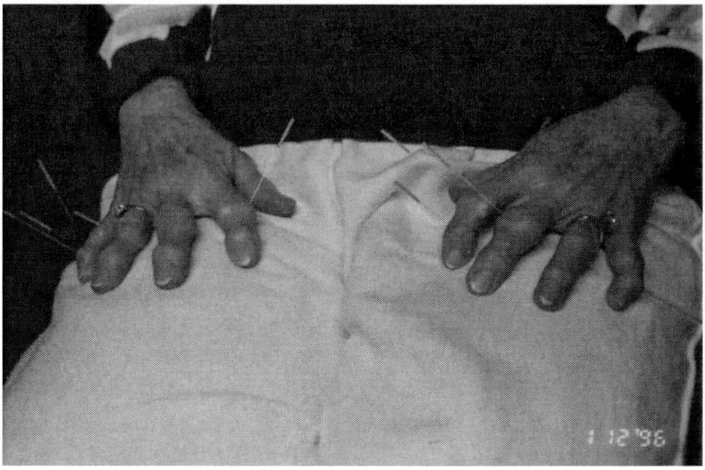

Figure 6. Patient receiving acupuncture for the pain of her arthritis.

NEW VITALITY

Once someone is out of pain, they often will feel they are back to normal and want to stop their treatment plan. It is normal to feel this way. It's like seeing the light at the end of a long tunnel you have just crawled through. You will notice that you feel better when arising. You sleep better thus you feel better and have more energy.

In general, you may feel now that your life is worth living again you want this feeling to continue, this is the stage you need to talk to the practitioner and discuss with them a maintenance plan to continue feeling the quality of life you thought you had lost just because you have become a senior.

The point is not to only eliminate pain but to get you to where you again enjoy life, dancing, golf, going to parties, travel and playing with grandchildren. You want your life to be worth living and by the focus of your life going from disease and illness to maintenance and wellness your new focus will keep your health compass true.

MAINTENANCE CARE

Maintenance starts with good nutrition and lifestyle, these will be two areas you will discuss when starting your maintenance program because of the focus on your wellness and prevention. A study conducted in 2001 showed a person enrolled in a health and wellness maintenance program had a 70% lower chance of being under the care of a nursing home than those seniors not enrolled in a maintenance program.

Remaining home, rather than having to be cared for by others in a convalescent facility is preferable to most seniors and that is our feeling as well.

Chapter XII

TREATMENT, CARE AND PHILOSOPHY

"Kindness in words creates confidence.
Kindness in thinking creates profoundness.
Kindness in giving creates love."

LAO-TZU (c. 4th century BC)

A WELLNESS CONCEPT

As a patient when you first go to a holistic care provider you want to know their basic health and wellness philosophy. Some Integrative Medicine practices were established nearly 40 years ago in order for doctors and patients with a similar viewpoint to be able to come together to discuss, consult and care for health conditions of their patients in a way that minimizes the need medication and/or surgery.

When you decide on this method of care and make your first appointment you will fill out a patient health history and then review it with the Integrative practitioner. After the initial consultation where you explain your problems, there is a thorough examination. The practitioner will use diagnostic testing methods, some of which you will be familiar with and others you may not be.

Most of the tests will be done in office or the practitioner will send you out to another facility for further tests or imaging. Some of the tests are radiographs, MRI's, CAT scans, and Nerve Conduction Velocity (NCV), electromyography (EMG), Computerized Trace Mineral Analysis (Hair analysis) and or Serology (Blood analysis) are a few that could be requested in addition to these but they are rare. In most cases the records from your family MD will suffice.

Three Phases of Care

There are three phases of care for most people: initial intensive or relief care; rehabilitative and corrective care; and finally the maintenance and wellness care.

Initial Intensive

In this phase, the main goal and objective is to eliminate pain and stabilize your condition as soon as possible. Since pain is the last symptom to show its self and the first to resolve progress is usually seen rapidly.

Corrective and Rehabilitative Care

In this phase, the main goal is to increase strength, flexibility, muscle balance, coordination and energy. This phase of care is to prevent reoccurrence of the problem and stabilization of the condition.

Wellness Care

This phase of care starts when the other phases are finished and maintenance is the key component of care. The goal and objective is to teach the patient how to maintain wellness and health now obtained through good diligent work and care of the human mind, body, and spirit. Not everyone begins in the initial or corrective phase, because they don't wait until there is a problem to come in for care. They want to stay healthy and prevent problems before they occur. For those people that already think like this we applaud your foresight.

This preventive and wellness phase means that you basically can select how often you feel best coming in. Many of our patients feel best if they come in each month for a balancing acupuncture treatment and a chiropractic adjustment. Others wait three months and some six months. Most can go for six months because we know they are on a good nutrition and exercise program that will keep them well, healthy and happy until we can see them for a checkup. We have marathoners, triathletes and elite athletes like our football, rugby and tennis players that come in during their off season when there is no injury to be treated.

When there is an injury to be addressed, we make an assessment if are in the area. If they are in another city we try to follow the case as closely as possible and help in any way that we can until they return.

Treatment Modalities

There are many treatment modalities used in Integrative wellness care. Each practitioner evaluates the condition of the patient and determines the modality they find necessary to correct the imbalance, subluxation, misalignment, fixation, adhesion, strain, sprain, spasm, illness, condition or loss of energy found in the body.

Some of the modalities used are: electrical, ultrasound, laser (light energy), heat, cold, manipulation, massage, acupuncture, moxibustion, cupping, homeopathy, naturopathy, and various techniques of muscle and energy work like Applied Kinesiology, Craniosacral, as well as ART may be used to correct a problem. Usually, if it's taught one of your practitioners is familiar with the procedure. Like reflexology, even if we don't advertise it specifically our practitioners and therapist know it and use it when needed or requested.

Rehabilitative Exercises and Stretches

Each practitioner advises exercise and stretches for specific problems they are dealing with in each condition, some of the exercises are done in the office and some at home exercises are used until the patient becomes familiar with the procedure.

There are times when we work with physical trainers, physical therapists and massage therapists due to extenuating circumstances and space limitations. Exercise rehabilitation is a vital component to help restore the range of motion, strength, endurance, flexibility, and to prevent reoccurrences, relapses and prevent further progression of a condition. The rehabilitative exercises will vary according to the condition, patient, health status, age and activity levels expected.

You may be asked by your practitioner to begin exercises you have never attempted before like: Yoga, Tai Qi, Qigong or Pilates, etc., because these exercises have been found to be highly effective for some conditions such as low back, neck, shoulder and hip pain. Don't be surprised when your practitioner gets down on the floor and demonstrates the correct form not once but many times for your health benefit.

In Summary

- Keep your body mass index (BMI) under 25
- Exercise 30 minutes daily or at least 3.5 hours weekly.
- Emphasize a diet of plant-based whole foods and reduce your red meat consumption.
- Take vitamin D, Omega 3, multivitamin and a probiotic daily.
- Use some practice to keep yourself mentally, emotionally and spiritually balanced and centered, such as your religion, yoga, meditation, martial arts, etc.

This list corresponds very well with a recent study that was published in the *Archives of Internal Medicine.* People in that study who had all four of these factors (below) had a 78 percent lower risk of getting any chronic degenerative disease, including diabetes, cancer, stroke or heart disease.

- Never having smoked.
- Body mass index less than 30.
- Participated in a physical activity 3.5 hours or more each week.
- Healthy dietary principles, which included a high intake of whole fruits, vegetables and whole grain, as well as low meat consumption.

Consider adding vitamin D, Omega 3, a probiotic and a good quality multivitamin, to the above recommendations and it would further lower the risk of developing a chronic degenerative disease. The current system of spending so much money on pharmaceutical medications for problems would best be addressed by lifestyle factors we have discussed and natural therapeutics rather than continued pharmaceutical research. Increasing the recognition of integrative wellness and preventive medicine and lifestyle in our health care system will play a more and more prominent role in the future of wellness care in our country. We hope with this book and some of the suggestions the paradigm shift will take us from a disease-care system to one of a true proactive prevention system of wellness and true health care.

There is a great deal more that we would like to cover in this book but time and space prevents us from continuing on for another hundred pages. If you will take this information and apply just half you will be far ahead of the game of health, wellness and lifestyle management.

Chapter XIII

PREVENTION AND WELLNESS FUNDING

"I am still determined to be cheerful and happy, in whatever situation I may be; for I have also learned from experience that the greater part of our happiness or misery depends upon our dispositions, and not upon our circumstances."

MARTHA WASHINGTON (1732- 1802)

In 2005, Senator Tom Harkin of Iowa said: "Let's face it, in America today we don't have a health care system, we have a sick care system. We wait until people become obese, develop chronic disease or become disabled – and then we spend untold hundreds of billions annually to try to make them better." Nearly a decade later, Senator Harkin has authored a spending package that provides close to $1 billion for prevention and Public Health Fund (Section 4002 of the Affordable Care Act). The U.S. senate approved the bill on January 16, 2014.

According to the U.S. Department of Health and Human Services (HHS), the fund is an investment to "help control the obesity epidemic, fight health disparities, detect and quickly respond to health threats, and reduce tobacco use among other things." HHS also has stated the fund will provide programs to tackle primary causes of costly, preventable chronic disease, plus help prevent accidents and injuries.

Everyone's Role in Public Health and Prevention

Most of the Integrative practitioners have long helped the nation toward meeting Healthy People 2020's health objectives without knowing it. These objectives include but are not limited to:

a) Reducing activity limitations due to chronic musculoskeletal conditions.
b) Improving health-related quality of life and well-being for all individuals.
c) Increasing the proportion of doctor office visits that include counseling or education related to physical activity (exercise).
d) Reducing tobacco use by teenagers and adults.

Imagine being funded or reimbursed for preventive care and services we have been discussing. The organization exists. It's called the American Public Health Association (APHA). Support and communicate with members of this organization that is fighting for your rights to health by prevention and wellness methods. Join the APHA as a citizen and have a voice in your future health care.

It's All About Life Style Management

At a recent conference at the meeting of the Academy of Anti-Aging Medicine (A4M) held May 2014 in Orlando, Florida, with more than 2,000 Physician and health care workers attending, health and preventative medicine experts presented different aspects of understanding and utilizing Integrative Medicine. Attendees had the opportunity to hear preventive medicine expert David Katz, MD, MPH, FACP, deliver the keynote address covering the topic of "Integrative Medicine: A Bridge Over Healthcare's Troubled Waters." Dr. Katz, a champion in the push for Integrative Medicine and founding director of Yale University's Prevention Research Center, was quoted as saying, "you can't stop the clock in regards to aging, but we do have the retention power to improve how we live and physicians and health care professionals need to make sure this information gets to our patients so they can have the freedom of choices when it comes to healthy living and lifestyle options."

This reiterates the critical role diet, nutrition, exercise and lifestyle play in the grand scheme of avoiding obesity, diabetes, heart disease and cancer. The Centers of Disease Control (CDC) has stated that one in three adults in the U.S. will have diabetes by the year 2050 if our lifestyles don't change.

The challenge is in achieving cooperation among health care practitioners to achieve the balance needed between crisis care management and health and wellness care. For many years conventional medicine and pharmacology had no competition in the health market place. This new century has spurred innovation and a fresh look at prevention and wellness care. Wellness and Prevention are different types of health care and require a different orientation than the public has been used to for years.

Today the public is a much more educated and sophisticated about their health care and willing to make informed decisions based on an entire set of circumstances, than were present in the past one hundred years. This new century has brought us into a contemporary and modern world of Wellness Care, so let's be sure we use what is available to help us.

References

Anderson S.S and Anderson, M.R. Why Your Doctor Offers Nutritional Supplements. *Selene River Press,* Ft Collins, CO. 2010.

Anderson S.S. Put Your Money Where Your Mouth Is! *Selene River Press,* Ft Collins, CO, 2005.

Bittman M. Food Matters. *Simon and Schuster,* New York, 2009.

Bland J. The Disease Delusion: Conquering the Causes of Illness for a Healthier, Longer and Happier Life. *HarperWave*, 2014.

Booth K.A. and Wyman T.D. Anatomy, Physiology and Pathophysiology for Allied Health. *McGraw Hill,* New York, 2008.

Cargill M. Acupuncture. *Praeger,* London, 1994.

Cullen E. Normal Blood Test Scores Aren't Good Enough. *YFH Press*, Tavares, FL 2003.

Cuthbert S. Applied Kinesiology Essentials: The Missing Link in Healthcare. *Gangases Press, 2013.*

Deadman P, Al-Khafaji M, and Baker K. A Manual of Acupuncture. *Journal of Chinese Medicine Publications,* East Sussex, England, 2001.

DeCava J. The Real Truth About Vitamins. *Selene River Press*. Loveland, CO. 2006.

Dobberstein L. Osteoarthritis: What kinds of oils are in your joints? *Nutritional Perspectives*, Vol 37, No. 3, 2014.

Egger, G. In Search of a Germ Theory Equivalent for Chronic Disease. *Preventing Chronic Disease*, 9, 2012.

Feuling T.J. Chiropractic Works. *Wellness Solutions,* 1999.

Forleo J. Health is Simple Disease is Complicated. *North Atlantic Books,* Berkeley, 2008.

Frost M. Back to the Basics of Human Health. *Expansive Health Awareness*, Inc. 2007.

Grant D. Inflammation The #1 Cause of Disease. *The American Chiropractor.* September 2014. P.44-48. www.amchiropractor.com

Gerber R. Vibrational Medicine for the 21st Century. *Eagle Brook*, New York. 2000.

Hawk C, et al. (2010). "Best practices recommendations for chiropractic care for older adults: results of a consensus process." *J. Manipulation Physiol Ther* 33(6): 464-473.

Hyman M. The Blood Sugar Solution. *Little, Brown and Company,* New York. 2012.

Keeney BJ, et al. (2013). "Early Predictors of Lumbar Spine Surgery After Occupational Back Injury: Results from a Prospective Study of Workers in Washington State." *Spine* (Phila PA 1986) 38(11): 953-964.

King F. Vital Energy in Life and Medicine. *The American Chiropractor,* September 2014, pp. 19-20. www.amchiropractor.com

Maciocia G. The Foundations of Chinese Medicine. *Churchill Livingstone*, London, 1989.

Masarsky and Todres-Masarsky. Somatovisceral Aspects of Chiropractic. *Churchill Livingstone*, New York, 2001.

Mayor D and Micozzi M. Energy Medicine East and West. *Churchill Livingstone,* 2011.

McTaggart L. The Field. *Harper*, New York, 1987.

Medford L. Why Do I Need Whole Food Supplements. *LND Publishing,* Tulsa, 2002.

Merritt M. Your Gut: Why you should be very afraid. *Nutritional Wellness*, May 2014, Vol 10, No. 2.

Micozzi M. Foundations of Complementary and Alternative Medicine. *Sunders-Elsevier*, St Louis, MO, 2011.

Moalem S. Survival of the Sickest. *William Morrow*. 2007

Morter T.M. Your Health Your Choice. *Fell Publishers, Inc.*, Hollywood, FL, 1990.

Nicolas P. The Best Kept Secret to Neck and Back Pain. *FBP, 2010.*

Petersen D. Love a Nurse and they'll love you back. *Dynamic Chiropractic*, Sept 1, 2014.

Powell RA. Medical Dramas. *Readers Digest.* March 2014, P.68.

Reston, J. Now, About My Operation in Peking. *New York Times*, July 26, 1971

Roizen MF and Oz MC. You: the Owner's Manual. *Harper Resource*, 2005.

Rosner A. *Dynamic Chiropractic*. July 1, 2014, Vol 32, Issue 13.

Rothfeld GS and Levert S. The Acupuncture Response. *Contemporary Books, McGraw-Hill*, New York, 2002.

Rubin J. The Great Physician's Rx for Health & Wellness. *Nelson Books*. 2006.

Saeger J.L. and Kyle-Brown D. New Foundations in Therapeutic Massage and Bodywork. *McGraw-Hill,* New York, 2008.

Seaman D. Putting Meat into Perspective. *Nutritional Wellness*. May 2014, Vol. 10, No. 2.

Stone J. Take Two Apples and Call Me in the Morning. *Hara.* Seattle, WA, 2003.

Stump JL. A Stroke of Midnight. *Alternative Concepts Publishing*. 2007.

Strand RD. Death By Prescription. *Thomas Nelson Publishers*, Nashville, 2003.

Stux G. and Pomeranz B. Basics of Acupuncture. *Springer-Verlag,* London, 1991.

Trupo G. How Chiropractic Helps You! *Totally Booked Practice, 2011.*

Waddell D. Longevity Utilizing Acupuncture, Chinese Medicine, Dietary and Life Style Changes. *Natural Practitioner Journal,* May 2014. www.naturalpractitionermag.com

Walters C. Minerals for the Genetic Code. *Acres USA*, Austin, TX, 2006.

Weil A. Health and Healing. *Houghton Mifflin Company,* New York, 1998.

Wild D.B. The Skin, Tongue and Nails Speak. *Selene River Press,* Loveland, CO, 2012.

Williams T. Chinese Medicine. *Element,* Queensland, 1996.

Yun-Tao Ma, Mila Ma, Zang Hee Cho. Biomedical Acupuncture for Pain Management. *Elsevier Churchill Livingstone*, St Louis, 2005.

Zukav G. The Dancing Wu Li Masters. *Quill William Morrow*, New York, 1979.

Other Resources

The University of Arizona Center for Integrative Medicine
Tucson, AZ - 520-626-6417- www.azcim.org.

American College of Healthcare Sciences
Portland, OR – 503- 244-0726 – www.achs.edu

Bastyr University
Kenmore, WA – 425-602-3000 – www.bastyr.edu

Anti-Aging, Regenerative and Functional Medicine information contact: www.a4m.com

Northwestern Health Sciences University
Bloomington, Minnesota, (a suburb of Minneapolis)
2501 W 84th St, Bloomington, MN 55431
(952) 888-4777
www.NorthwesternHealthSciencesUniversity.edu

INTEGRATIVE PRACTITIONERS/CONSULTANTS

David P. Sniezek, MD
McLean, VA 22101
Sniezek@aol.com

Lissa Rankin, MD
www.lissarankin.com
www.mindovermedicine.com

Mariah Stump, MD
Brown University College of Women
Department of Integrative Medicine
Providence, RI 02906

AUTHOR'S CONTACT INFORMATION

Dr. John Stump, DC, PhD, EdD
Director
Integrative Medicine Centre
Fairhope, Alabama, United States

Dr. Donna Retzlaff-Roberts, PhD
University of South Alabama
Mobile, Alabama, United States
Email: retzlaff@southalabama.edu

Dr. David P. Sniezek, DC, MD, Lac
Attending Staff
National Medical Center
Washington DC, United States

INDEX

#

A

B

C

D

E

F

J

K

L

M

N

O

P

Q

R

S

T

U

V

W

X

Y

Z